A Humanistic Approach to English for Academic Purposes Pedagogy

Laura Dyer

A Humanistic Approach to English for Academic Purposes Pedagogy

People, Place, Compassion, Power

palgrave
macmillan

Laura Dyer
Language Centre
University of Leeds
Leeds, UK

ISBN 978-3-032-00185-6 ISBN 978-3-032-00186-3 (eBook)
https://doi.org/10.1007/978-3-032-00186-3

Cover credit line: Jacob Lund/Alamy Stock Photo

This Palgrave Macmillan imprint is published by the registered company Springer Nature Switzerland AG
The registered company address is: Gewerbestrasse 11, 6330 Cham, Switzerland

Acknowledgements I would like to thank the following people for sharing their knowledge and/or peer reviewing individual chapters:

Michelle Evans (University of Leeds)
Natalia Fedorova (Universidade de Coimbra)
Kashmir Kaur (University of Leeds)
Thuy Thai (University of Leeds)

Competing Interests The author has no competing interests to declare that are relevant to the content of this manuscript.

Contents

Glossary of Acronyms

AI	Artificial Intelligence
BALEAP	British Association of Lecturers in English for Academic Purposes. A professional organisation for practitioners working in the field of EAP
CEFR	Common European Framework of Reference for Languages. A set of descriptors determining linguistic competency levels
CoP	Community of Practice. A group of people who come together sharing a common interest or goal
CPD	Continuing Professional Development
EAP	English for Academic Purposes
EGAP	English for General Academic Purposes
ELT	English Language Teaching
EMI	English as a Medium of Instruction
ESAP	English for Specific Academic Purposes
GPA	Grade Point Average. A number representing the average score from a student's accumulated scores
HE	Higher Education
HEI	Higher Education Institution
IELTS	International English Language Testing System. An exam for testing English language competency that is accepted

	internationally for entry to academic studies through the English language
IFP	International Foundation Programme
ISP	In-Sessional Programme
K-12	Kindergarten to 12th grade. A programme of compulsory public schooling based on the American education system and adopted by many countries and institutions worldwide. It is a programme that provides twelve years of schooling
L1	First Language
PPCP	People, Place, Compassion, Power. The humanistic theory for the planning and designing of pedagogical activities that is presented in this book
PSP	Pre-Sessional Programme
PTA	Protagonists, Thoughts and Approaches. An acronym created specifically for this publication to collectively refer to those persons and ideas linked to humanistic ideology
SCT	Socio-Cultural Theory
STEM	Science, Technology, Engineering and Mathematics
SW	The Silent Way
TBL	Task-Based Learning
TNE	Trans-National Education
TOEFL	Test Of English as a Foreign Language. An exam for testing English language competency that is accepted internationally for entry to academic studies through the English language
TOEIC	Test Of English for International Communication. An exam for testing English language competency that is accepted internationally for entry to academic studies through the English language
UKPSF	United Kingdom Professional Standards Framework
ZPD	Zones of Proximal Development

List of Figures

List of Tables

1

Determining the Purpose of This Publication, the Purpose of EAP and the Potential of Humanism in Its Practice

1.1 A Learning Experience?

This is a book about pedagogy, specifically a theory created for the purpose of designing and planning of pedagogical activities in the field of EAP. It is a book that places the learner at the centre of learning process and places emphasis on the importance of emotions and the individual in learning achievement. It is not a book that provides the practitioner with a mechanistic outline of how to teach EAP, rather it asks them to consider how to provide a more positive learning experience for the student through the application of a theory for the designing and planning process. In understanding the purpose of this book, I ask the reader to place themselves in the following scenario involving two EAP students which I will name Lee and Jo:

Lee is asked to deliver a fifteen minute presentation, but the topic of the presentation is one that Lee has limited knowledge of. The topic is to be presented to an audience of peers and teachers who will ask questions at the end about its content. All of this will take place in English which is not Lee's first language.

- How would you feel if you were Lee?

L. Dyer, *A Humanistic Approach to English for Academic Purposes Pedagogy*,
https://doi.org/10.1007/978-3-032-00186-3_1

- What aspects of this task could be challenging for you?
- How would you feel about this task if you had never done a presentation before?

Moving on to Jo who is allocated the task of providing peer feedback to Lee on their presentation. This is to be done verbally in front of the presentation audience immediately after Lee has finished presenting and answering questions.

- How would you feel if you were Jo?
- Would you be honest if you felt that Lee's presentation was not successful?
- What if you did not understand Lee's presentation but it appears that other audience members did?
- How would you feel if you were unable to provide quality feedback?
- How would you feel if you were Lee and Jo expressed negative views about your presentation in front of the audience?

In this context both Lee and Jo are under pressure to 'perform' for an audience and the pressure of the situation may impact on the performance of both students. It is likely that both students will encounter difficulties in their performances, leading to issues with their output which may not be a true reflection of their capabilities. This book presents People, Place, Compassion, Power (PPCP) as a means to help mitigate situations such as these in order to provide a more positive experience for the learner. As will be highlighted throughout this book, EAP and its learners have multiple pathways to navigate in order to achieve the outcomes that institutions and practitioners set. Through changes in how pedagogical activities are delivered, the learning experience can be optimised to produce a more positive learning experience. This in turn could increase the likelihood of positive outcomes (see Chapter 2). It is hoped that this book will encourage a more inclusive, engaging and increased sense of belonging in EAP pedagogical activities.

1.2 The Evolution of EAP

Before continuing, it is important to outline what is meant by 'EAP'. The evolution of EAP can be split into five stages, as shown in Fig. 1.1: support, emergence, development, investigative and recognition.

The support stage can be traced back to the 1960s. Here EAP developed in Western English-speaking HE as a means to enable learners from outside that context to integrate and participate academically within those institutions. As such it took on a supporting role in readying students for their academic disciplinary work. In the support stage EAP focused on the analysis and application of linguistic features of English, specifically in the scientific field (Benesch 2001). The emergence stage occurred during the 1970s with a specific focus on rhetorical analysis (Benesch 2001). It is at this stage that EAP progressed from being a support mechanism to a field where knowledge began to accumulate. The development stages saw EAP expand into the study skills and needs analysis arenas in the 1980s and discourse analysis in the 1990s (Benesch 2001). Here EAP moved from the 'one size fits all approach' to tailored learning approaches whilst opening the door to potential scholarly activities. The twenty-first century saw the investigative stage strengthen the scholarly aspect of EAP, which enlarged to an extent that EAP journals such as the *Journal of English for Academic Purposes* were set up for the dissemination of output. It was also here that professional organisations such as BALEAP appeared to support the growth of EAP the discipline of EAP (Ding and Bruce 2017). This was followed by the recognition stage of EAP with the realisation of professional training specifically for EAP. This is evidenced through schemes such as BALEAP's teaching excellence framework (BALEAP 2024) and EAP practitioner training qualifications materialised (BALEAP 2025). From this timeline it can be

Support → Emergence → Development → Investigative → Recognition

Fig. 1.1 The evolution of EAP

seen how EAP initially developed as a support mechanism for students in specific contexts before expanding into its own theoretical research practice (Hyland and Shaw 2016) and professional development schemes. This development has led to the separation of EAP into two components in which practitioners may participate. The first component is the student facing pedagogical one and the second is the desk-based research one. It is the pedagogical component which has led to EAP's development as a discipline within its own right through the dissemination of knowledge from desk-based research by its practitioners. The growth in EAP has undoubtedly brought to light new openings and perspectives for practitioners to demonstrate their skills and knowledge and rightly gain the recognition that other 'traditional' disciplines have had for many years. This is evidenced by the ever-increasing amount of literature and organisations in the field (Webster 2022). Yet despite these advancements in the discipline of EAP, the Covid-19 pandemic brought a renewed focus on pedagogy and the learning process (BALEAP 2021), both of which drive the core principles of this publication.

1.3 The Form and Purpose of EAP

EAP is considered to be a branch of English for Specific Purposes which is part of the broader discipline of applied linguistics. EAP developed as a result of the recognition of the need to train learners in language that could be considered most useful for their context (Charles and Pecorari 2015). EAP itself can be split further into EGAP and ESAP, both of which are discussed in Sect. 3.3.2. Whilst there is no strict definition of what EAP is (Li 2017), in general it could be said that it is a learning experience that shares many similarities with English language teaching but with a focus on academic rather than general language (Kostka and Olmstead-Wang 2014). Through EAP's curricula it can be surmised that pedagogy surrounding EAP is not one that focuses on content but rather on skills as it is delivered as preparatory or support for academic studies. The content of an EAP curriculum therefore is different to the curricula of other academic disciplines in that it is not focused on expanding subject knowledge. Instead it provides a foundation for the presentation of knowledge. It is from this 'different' curriculum and the EAP student being 'different' (see Sect. 4.1) that an EAP pedagogy emerges. It is through this pedagogy that the EAP learning experience becomes one which can enable the student to successfully communicate and participate in their desired educational context (Ding and Bruce 2017; Bruce 2015). EAP is widely to be considered a twofold learning experience, with focus on language and academic skills development for a specified educational context (Ding and Bruce 2017; Hyland 2016; Charles and Pecorari 2015; Kostka and Olmstead-Wang 2014). Success in EAP is determined by the learner's ability to use these acquirements in their academic studies (James 2023) and it cannot be denied that for an EAP learner, the ability to apply these acquired skills to their academic studies can help to facilitate studies in their academic field. These attained skills can be determined by a range of factors such discipline, level and institution. For example, the language and skills deemed necessary for a university research postgraduate student in a STEM discipline is likely to differ from that of a high school student in an arts discipline. However, although EAP's purpose is to prepare students for academic studies, this takes place in a controlled situation which may not reflect reality. Being able to use the language and skills from EAP does not always equal subsequent success. Academic study is not just about the process and production of academic output but also the ability to participate in the academic community outside curriculum and assessment. It is for this reason that I suggest a third aspect to the purpose of EAP and that is to facilitate the academic studies learning experience by raising awareness of non-academic practices. These institutional academic practices refer to contexts which may not be directly related to curriculum and assessment but in which the student may be required to participate during their academic studies. Institutional academic practices could include being able to use any digital platforms employed by the institution, understanding institutional practices around the use of AI and being able to communicate verbally in unstructured situations. As practitioners we may consider ourselves to be successful if our learners achieve the language and skills components delivered in a PSP. But if the learner is not aware of what to expect once they progress to academic studies, they may resort to coping strategies to deal with negative experiences (Compas et al. 2006 cited in Surachman and Almeida 2018). This in turn can interrupt the learning experience (Feigenbaum 2024) and potentially nullify the fruits of EAP study. EAP should aim to prepare students for institutional academic practices and the wider academic community (Kostka and Olmstead-Wang 2014) and this can only be done if the learner 'knows what they are getting themselves into'. It is about preparing students for the 'real world' of their life as a student undertaking a programme of academic studies. From this, I propose the third purpose of EAP which is termed community skills in reference to the academic community the learner may join or is currently part of. These community skills are important in terms of facilitating transition to academic study and joining an academic community. Bruce (2015) outlines three organised communities in academic contexts, these are: speech communities, discourse communities and CoPs. A speech community refers to a group who share commonality in language, interpretation of language and contextualisation of language. Discourse communities are used to describe those who share common goals which are achieved through the community's conventions for discourse, particularly in written genres. The term CoP is applied to a group which is operating in similar conditions to achieve a specific goal. When reviewing community skills for EAP, it is important to consider each of these three components and how the implementation of these could be beneficial in contemporaneous and future learning processes. The three purposes of EAP are thus summarised with some example activities in Table 1.1.

1.4 The Title of This Publication

The title of this publication can be split into three parts:

- A humanistic approach
- English for Academic Purposes pedagogy
- People, place, compassion, power

Table 1.1 The three purposes of EAP with example activities

Purpose of EAP	Example activities
A. Bridging the perceived language gap of what is considered a language deficit between completed studies and future studies in the English language (BALEAP, n.d.)	• Summary writing • Paraphrasing • Academic vocabulary development (Coxhead 2000)
B. Raising consciousness and fostering the designated skills deemed necessary for academic study (Kostka and Olmstead-Wang 2014; BALEAP, n.d.)	• Critical reading (Wilson 2016) • Presentation skills • Referencing
C. Raising awareness of community skills	• Exploring content of intended future study programmes • Examining communication genres considered useful for academic study such as email (Du-Babcock and Feng 2018) • Developing spoken communication with a focus on communicating in unstructured academic contexts such personal tutorials and with departmental staff such as lab technicians or administrators

A 'humanistic approach' is the key focus of this publication which refers to humanistic approaches in education. Stemming from psychology, a humanistic approach prioritises developing the individual as a whole being and not just the accumulation of subject knowledge. Humanistic approaches, often known as humanistic learning theory, take into account the importance of emotions in the learning process and how these can impact on the learning experience.

English for academic purposes pedagogy refers to the pedagogy that is specific to EAP. That is one that supports the commonly viewed purposes A and B outlined in Table 1.1. The humanistic approach to pedagogy in this publication seeks to provide an engaging learning experience in an environment that supports autonomy, self-reflection and allows for student-centred learning.

People, place, compassion, power refers to the theory presented in this publication. It is a theory for practitioners to use in their development of pedagogical activities with specific reference to EAP. The theory outlines three components determined by educators—people, place and compassion. People considers the dynamics of the learning space and how this can impact on the learner's potential to acquire language. Place factors in how the learning environment can impact on a student's progress. The implementation of compassion in pedagogical activities may direct the learner away from 'traditional' academic achievement. But without compassion we are unable to help the learner (Waddington 2016) and run the risk of fostering negative emotions (Maxwell 2017) which in the long run may too move the learner away from academic achievement. These three components—people, place and compassion—ask educators to consider if and how these may applied to pedagogical activities. The final component, power, is demonstrated by the learner should the conditions the teacher determined components be met. PPCP is designed to be used by educators to create a more humanistic learning experience for the learner.

In addition to the three parts above, this publication includes a compendium of activities that links with PPCP theory.

Whilst the four components of PPCP have been studied extensively independently in regard to EAP, (see for example Asoodar et al. 2014 for online CoPs, Bunch and Watson (2024) on critical care in EAP and Dhillon and Murray (2021) on the use of technological places of study), they have not previously been brought together for the educator to consider as a whole in their practice.

1.5 Why Use a Humanistic Approach in EAP?

A variety of approaches exist in EAP course design. Examples include:

- *Content based*: where a course is designed around specific content with target language aims (Brinton, Snow and Wesche 2003 cited in James 2006). An example of this includes the emergence of discipline specific PSPs where course content is chosen to ease the transfer of learning from EAP to academic studies.

- *Task based*: where activities are chosen to replicate what students may experience in their academic studies (Douglas and Kim 2014). Tasks may include listening to lectures and participating in seminars.
- *Project based*: an expansion of task based where a sustained pedagogical activity is carried out to replicate that of projects in academic studies (Abdullah et al. 2022).

However, a humanistic approach has yet to significantly impact on the forefront of EAP course design. A humanistic approach to education is nothing new, with concepts such as Rogers' student-centred learning (see Chapter 2) having become part of mainstream pedagogy, yet humanism is an approach that is not widely used. This publication demonstrates that a humanistic approach to EAP, specifically its pedagogical design, could prove beneficial for learners. PPCP developed from the application of humanistic approaches to the designing and planning of pedagogical activities to place the learners at the heart of the EAP experience. It can be said to be a more compassionate approach to education. Designing and planning of pedagogical activities enables the teacher to provide structure in the learning process. It acknowledges that needs differ from learner to learner and that the profile of learners evolves over time (Advance HE et al. 2023). PPCP recognises individual characteristics of the individual learner. Through the application of PPCP, the learner has the opportunity to demonstrate their ability and potential in their EAP studies. PPCP draws attention to the fact that EAP learners are different from other 'regular subject' learners due to the nature and purpose of EAP. Whereas a 'regular subject' such as history or civil engineering may provide students with knowledge and skills based around content, EAP deconstructs the learning process to consider why and how knowledge is presented in a particular manner. However, approaches to pedagogy may not always take the individual into account. For example, instructional EAP literature generally focuses on the expected output and how to get there through scaffolding. However, it does not consider how students feel if they struggle to meet expectations at any point during their training. One such example of this is the action of showing students examples of previous learners' work. Whilst there are many benefits to this such as raising student awareness of the type of work we expect from them which may indeed help focus and guide some learners, seeing 'good' work may have a detrimental effect on those who may feel overwhelmed at the prospect of creating such output. This could have a negative effect on emotions and potential learning outcomes (see Sect. 2.6.2.5).

EAP can prove to be a stressful and anxiety inducing experience (Wilson 2016). The use of English in academia requires engagement in high level cognitive processing alongside the use of discourse which could be considered challenging even for an L1 speaker (Charles and Pecorari 2015). Thus steps must be taken to reduce these negative emotions which could prove damaging to the learning process. As outlined in the example in Sect. 1.1, learners, both EAP and non-EAP, could experience negative emotions that can affect their learning experiences and outcomes. EAP developed in a Western context where educational socialisation practices promoted self-expression (Pearson and Podeschi 1999), linking with Maslow's concepts of self-identity and autonomy as a means of self-development and actualisation (see Sect. 2.6.1.2). However, if a learner undertakes EAP having not previously experienced such educational socialisation practices, they may face difficulties adapting to or adopting this approach. This may cause an interruption to their learning process and the possibility that they may not be able to reach their full potential. This is because the learner may experience an inhibiting 'coping' behaviour rather than an intrinsically motivated 'expressive' behaviour (Maslow 1954 cited in DeCarvalho 1991). This in turn can have a negative impact on an individual student's learning experience and output as they attempt to navigate the divergent approaches to education alongside course requirements.

EAP PSPs are frequently viewed from a deficit perspective in that they are seen as being for learners who are weaker linguistically and in terms of skills (Pearson 2020). As such, EAP could be considered an oppressor to the students who are restricted from showing their realities (Freire 1993). This notion of deficit, as a result of oppression, is often placed on the learner rather than the educational training they have received (Wallace 2015). This is often reflected in EAP pedagogy which has long been concerned with moulding learners into the desired academic 'norm' for the context they are in. However, it does not take into account how learners may feel when undertaking this reshaping of their construct. Emotions are central to a learner's educational pathway and impact on both their well-being and mental health (Pekrun 2006). If a learner experiences a negative emotional state, this may impact on their eventual learning outcomes. EAP frequently does not appreciate the knowledge and skills that a learner already has. Instead it takes a back-to-basics approach with learners (*e.g. this is how you structure a paragraph, this is how you take notes...*) rather than discovering what the learner already knows and allowing them to use that knowledge. This approach has the potential to direct learners into a level of self-perceived deficit, placing them under pressure to perform to the standards that 'we' have set through English language testing examinations to gain entry to institutions, rather than discovering whether they can already meet those standards. As practitioners we should instead take a more liberal, welcoming approach that shares and builds on existing knowledge, experiences and skills. Although BALEAP highlighted a post-pandemic renewed interested in EAP pedagogy (BALEAP 2021), it is noticeable that it remains an undervalued topic with limited understanding on how it may impact on students (Hyland 2018). Likewise although humanism has had some discussion in the wider ELT context (see Gadd 1998), it remains an approach that is under researched and underexplored. To reignite the pedagogical aspect of EAP, it is suggested that taking humanistic approach to its pedagogy has the potential to provide a more positive learning experience for the students. A humanistic approach has the potential to develop all three of the purposes of EAP outlined in Table 1.1. This is because it allows for development of language through skills in developing reflection, dialogue and a socially equal approach between educators and learners (Al-Obaydi 2021).

This publication focuses on a humanistic approach to EAP pedagogy, yet there are crossovers with holistic education. In holistic education the aim is to educate the whole person, seeking to address emotional well-being alongside academic needs (American University 2020). This is also covered by humanistic approaches, but the main difference lies in the holistic approach to directly educate students in this way whereas a humanistic approach encourages these experiences through self-discovery. Through PPCP and a humanistic approach, the EAP student has the chance to develop the whole being alongside the academic through the conditions and opportunities provided to them to facilitate the transition to academic studies.

1.6 Using PPCP

PPCP was designed for use by practitioners in the designing and planning stage of pedagogical activities. However, it is recognised that it can be applied at other phases of the teaching and learning process. Phases in the teaching and learning process are outlined in the UKPSF which is a framework for the delivery of HE teaching and learning (Advance HE et al. 2023). The UKPSF outlines five areas of activity for those teaching and supporting learning in the area of HE. These five areas are:

- A1 design and plan learning activities and/or programmes
- A2 teach and/or support learning through appropriate approaches and environments
- A3 assess and give feedback for learning
- A4 support and guide learners
- A5 enhance practice through own professional development

(Advance HE et al. 2023, p. 5)

As previously stated, PPCP is strongly linked with A1 in that it asks educators to use PPCP in their designing and planning of pedagogical activities. It is at this early stage that educators can take the time to consider the content of their lessons before putting them into action in the classroom. It is at this stage where PPCP could be considered most useful. However, PPCP is also applicable to the other areas of activity. For example it links with A2 as it may also be applied when teaching and learning activities are in action and real-time adjustments could be made. A2 also stresses the importance of the learning environment which is one of the key aspects of PPCP through the 'place' component. For A3 PPCP can be applied to support a more compassionate approach to assessing learning and this is evidenced through activities which can be found in the compendium. PPCP connects strongly with A4 in that as it is a humanistic theory, it aims to provide learning conditions that are supportive for students. Whilst there is less connection to A5, PPCP may be used by practitioners as a means to enhance CPD through an alternative approach to pedagogy.

1.7 An Alternative Approach to EAP Pedagogy

The purpose of this publication and PPCP is not to dismiss existing EAP pedagogy, but to encourage practitioners to recognise the individual learner. Through the presentation of PPCP practitioners have the chance to consider if adaptations to existing activities, creation of new ones or simply valuing existing ones in their teaching could benefit the learning experience. It is recognised that an all-encompassing application of PPCP to EAP curricula may be too complex to apply, time consuming or even a hindrance to achieving learning objectives. However, what this book does call for is for the learner and their experiences to be placed at the forefront and to be able to demonstrate new or existing attributes by considering and fostering conducive learning conditions. Whilst learners are accepting of a traditional approach to pedagogical activities, they are often more engaged and receptive to more innovative approaches (Meguid and Collins 2017; Wake et al. 2023). This in turn could prove beneficial for both learners who may need extra support and for those who may already be considered as 'successful'. Although each of the components of PPCP have already been explored separately in EAP scholarly outputs, they have not been examined in a collectivised manner. This publication calls for the practitioner to return to the foundation of EAP—the pedagogy for learners undertaking or preparing to undertake academic studies in the English language. Without the learners themselves we would not have the opportunity to expand our knowledge and build EAP into the discipline it has become. PPCP is both a new perspective and a call for change in EAP pedagogy.

1.8 Overview of the Publication

The overview of the chapters of this book are as follows:

Chapter 2 looks at humanism and its use in education, providing a philosophical springboard for subsequent chapters. It considers key humanistic theories and approaches to education and outlines principles for the creation of EAP pedagogical activities.

Chapter 3 reviews the range of contexts in which EAP may take place. This sets the scene for how teachers may teach and students may learn. This will allow for practitioners to consider whether humanism can be applied to their own teaching context.

Following this, Chapter 4 considers who the EAP student is, the emotions involved in studying EAP, how they are different to 'regular' academic discipline students and issues they may face when undertaking their EAP studies. This chapter highlights the EAP students journey and why humanism could be beneficial.

Chapter 5 presents PPCP, looking at how it was conceived and each of the individual components that make up the theory.

Chapter 6 is a compendium of activities influenced by PPCP. These activities can be used by practitioners in their presented form, adapted to suit needs or be used as a starting point for the creation of further activities.

The final chapter of this publication provides a discussion on humanism in education, PPCP, information on PPCP's potential application outside EAP and concluding thoughts on the theory.

Being based in a UK HEI, many of the examples used in this book reflect learners in that context as it is the one I am most familiar with. However, I have also strived to include information from other global contexts to demonstrate EAP's influence worldwide.

1.9 Notes on Terminology

The term 'pedagogy' is taken from Greek to describe the educating of the young (Wallace 2015). As the majority of EAP occurs with older learners it could be said that the word 'andragogy' (the educating of adults) would be a more appropriate word to use in describing the function and content of this publication. However, as the word pedagogy is more widely used and accepted this is the term that is used throughout this publication in reference to the general act of educating.

The words 'learner' and 'student' are used interchangeably throughout this publication to provide variance in language.

The word 'teacher' may at times be interchanged with 'educator' and 'practitioner'. These three terms can refer to tutor, professor, lecturer or anyone involved with educating EAP learners.

Studies conducted outside EAP are referred to as 'academic studies' or 'disciplinary studies'. This could mean studies at undergraduate, taught postgraduate or research postgraduate, or potentially even K-12 level.

References

Abdullah, Hazlina, Haliza Harun, Nursyuhada Wahab, Suo Yan Juo, and Myra Aidrin Mohd Ali. 2022. Teaching English for academic purposes through project-based learning method and process writing approach. *International journal of languages and education* 1 (1). https://doi.org/10.33102/alazkiyaa.v1i1.8.

Advance HE, GuildHE, and Universities UK. 2023. Professional Standards Framework for teaching and supporting learning in higher education 2023. Advance HE, GuildHE, Universities UK. https://s3.eu-west-2.amazonaws.com/assets.creode.advancehe-document-manager/documents/advance-he/PSF%202023%20-%20Screen%20Reader%20Compatible%20-%20final_1675089549.pdf. Accessed 6 May 2024.

Al-Obaydi, Liqaa Habeb. 2021. Humanistic learning elements in a blended learning environment: A study in an EFL teaching context. *Interactive Learning Environments* 31 (5): 3098–3111. https://doi.org/10.1080/10494820.2021.1919717.

American University. 2020. What is holistic education? Understanding the history, methods, and benefits. https://soeonline.american.edu/blog/what-is-holistic-education/. Accessed 16 July 2025.

Asoodar, Maryam, Mahmood Reza Atai, Shahin Vaezi, and Seyedeh Susan Marandi. 2014. Examining effectiveness of communities of practice in online English for academic purposes (EAP) assessment in virtual classes.

Computers and Education 70: 291–300. https://doi.org/10.1016/j.compedu.2013.08.016.

BALEAP. 2021. The impact of Covid-19 on the UK EAP sector: An examination of how organisations delivering EAP were affected and responded in terms of academic delivery and operational procedures. https://www.baleap.org/wp-content/uploads/2021/06/BALEAP-Report-Covid-and-EAP-May-2021.pdf. Accessed 1 March 2025.

BALEAP. 2024. BALEAP TEAP individual accreditation scheme handbook 2024. https://www.baleap.org/wp-content/uploads/2024/10/BALEAP-TEAP-Handbook-2024-final-22-OCT-2024.pdf. Accessed 7 April 2024.

BALEAP. 2025. TEAP courses. https://www.baleap.org/resources/teap-courses. Accessed 7 April 2024.

BALEAP. n.d. BALEAP can do framework. Areas of competency within UK higher education, postgraduate level. https://www.baleap.org/wp-content/uploads/2016/04/Can_Do_Framework__with_sample_activities_April_2013.pdf. Accessed 18 February 2025.

Benesch, Sarah. 2001. *Critical English for academic purposes*. New York: Routledge.

Bruce, Ian. 2015. *Theory and concepts of English for academic purposes*. Basingstoke, Hampshire: Palgrave Macmillan.

Bunch, Philippa, and Lucy Watson. 2024. *Interlopers, collaborators, allies and resistance: The complex positioning of EAP tutors in the modern university*. Presentation at BALEAP PIM, King's College London, March. https://www.baleap.org/downloads/event-resources/2024-kcl/6.-bunch-and-watson-interlopers-collaborators-allies-and-resistance-the-complex-positioning-of-eap-tutors-inthe-modern-university.pdf

Charles, Maggie, and Diane Pecorari. 2015. *Introducing English for academic purposes*. London: Routledge. https://doi.org/10.4324/9781315682129.

Coxhead, Averil. 2000. A new academic word list. *TESOL Quarterly* 34 (2): 213–238. https://doi.org/10.2307/3587951.

DeCarvalho, Roy José. 1991. The humanistic paradigm in education. *The Humanistic Psychologist* 19 (1): 88–104. https://doi.org/10.1080/08873267.1991.9986754.

Dhillon, Sundeep, and Neil Murray. 2021. An investigation of EAP teachers' views and experiences of e-learning technology. *Education Sciences* 11 (2): 54. https://doi.org/10.3390/educsci11020054.

Ding, Alex, and Ian Bruce. 2017. *The English for academic purposes practitioner operating on the edge of academia*. Cham: Palgrave Macmillan.

Douglas, Scott Roy, and Marcia Kim. 2014. Task-based language teaching and English for Academic Purposes: An investigation into instructor perceptions and practice in the Canadian context. *TESL Canada Journal* 31 (1). https://eric.ed.gov/?id=EJ1052107.

Du-Babcock, Bertha, and Haiying Feng. 2018. Culture and identity on intercultural business requests: A genre-based comparative study. *Ibérica* 2: 171–200. https://www.researchgate.net/publication/324795677_Culture_and_identity_on_intercultural_business_requests_A_genre-based_comparative_study.

Feigenbaum, Kenneth D. 2024. A critique of Abraham Maslow and Carl Rogers as educators. *Journal of Humanistic Psychology* 64 (1): 44–63. https://doi.org/10.1177/00221678231154819.

Freire, Paulo. 1993. *Pedagogy of the oppressed*. Translated by Myra Berman Ramos. New York: Continuum.

Gadd, Nick. 1998. Towards less humanistic English teaching. *ELT Journal* 52 (3): 223–234.

Hyland, Ken. 2016. General and specific EAP. In *The Routledge handbook of English for academic purposes*, ed. Ken Hyland and Philip Shaw, 17–29. Abingdon: Routledge. https://doi.org/10.4324/9781315657455-2.

Hyland, Ken. 2018. Sympathy for the devil? A Defence of EAP. *Language Teaching* 51 (3): 383–399. https://doi.org/10.1017/S0261444818000101.

Hyland, Ken, and Philip Shaw. 2016. Introduction. In *The Routledge handbook of English for academic purposes*, ed. Ken Hyland and Philip Shaw, 1–14. Abingdon: Routledge. https://doi.org/10.4324/9781315657455-1.

James, Mark Andrew. 2006. Transfer of learning from a university content-based EAP course. *TESOL Quarterly* 40 (4): 783–806. https://doi.org/10.2307/40264308.

James, Mark A. 2023. An exploratory investigation of instructors' practices and challenges in promoting students' learning transfer in EAP education. *Journal of English for Academic Purposes* 64: 101263. https://doi.org/10.1016/j.jeap.2023.101263.

Kostka, Ilka, and Susan Olmstead-Wang. 2014. *Teaching English for academic purposes*. Chicago: TESOL Press.

Li, Yulong. 2017. What is EAP?—From multiple literacies to a humanistic paradigm shift. *Theory and Practice in Language Studies* 7 (7): 497–505. https://doi.org/10.17507/tpls.0707.01.

Maxwell, Bruce. 2017. Pursuing the aim of compassionate empathy in higher education. In *The pedagogy of compassion at the heart of higher education*, ed. Paul Gibbs, 33–49. Cham: Springer.

Meguid, Eiman Abdel, and Matthew Collins. 2017. Students' perceptions of lecturing approaches: Traditional versus interactive teaching. *Advances in Medical Education and Practice* 8: 229–240. https://doi.org/10.2147/AMEP.S131851.

Pearson, William S. 2020. The effectiveness of pre-sessional EAP programmes in UK higher education: A review of the evidence. *Review of Education* 8 (2): 420–447. https://doi.org/10.1002/rev3.3191.

Pearson, Elaine M., and Ronald L. Podeschi. 1999. Humanism and individualism: Maslow and his critics. *Adult Education Quarterly* 50 (1): 41–55. https://doi.org/10.1177/07417139922086902.

Pekrun, Reinhard. 2006. The control-value theory of achievement emotions: Assumptions, corollaries, and implications for educational research and practice. *Education Psychological Review* 18: 315–341. https://doi.org/10.1007/s10648-006-9029-9.

Surachman, Agus, and David M. Almeida. 2018. Stress and coping theory across the adult lifespan. *Oxford Research Encyclopedia of Psychology*. https://doi.org/10.1093/acrefore/9780190236557.013.341. Accessed 12 November 2024.

Waddington, Kathryn. 2016. The compassion gap in UK universities. *International Practice Development Journal* 6 (1): 10. https://doi.org/10.19043/ipdj.61.010.

Wake, Stephanie, Madeleine Pownall, Richard Harris, and Pam Birtill. 2023. Balancing pedagogical innovation with psychological safety? Student perceptions of authentic assessment. *Assessment and Evaluation in Higher Education* 49 (4): 511–522. https://doi.org/10.1080/02602938.2023.2275519.

Wallace, Susan. 2015. *A dictionary of education*, 2nd ed. Oxford: Oxford University Press.

Webster, Simon. 2022. The transition of EAP practitioners into scholarship writing. *Journal of English for Academic Purposes* 57: 101091. https://doi.org/10.1016/j.jeap.2022.101091.

Wilson, Kate. 2016. Critical reading, critical thinking: Delicate scaffolding in English for academic purposes (EAP). *Thinking Skills and Creativity* 22: 256–265. https://doi.org/10.1016/j.tsc.2016.10.002.

2

Humanism and Education

2.1 Overview of the Chapter

The purpose of this chapter is to look at the theoretical approaches in this publication's underpinning—that of humanism and how this can provide a positive outcome for the EAP student. It does not seek to develop argumentation both for and against humanistic ideology. Nor does it seek to provide an in-depth philosophical review of the significant range of humanistic theories and approaches that exist. Instead it looks at humanism from the eye of an EAP practitioner seeking to provide a positive learning experience for their students. Therefore this chapter explores humanism, its definitions and its development before moving on to how it has been applied in educational contexts. It then contemplates why humanism could prove beneficial for EAP pedagogy. Following this, a review of key humanistic PTAs to education is presented. Each of these are briefly examined and consideration is given as to how they can be applied to EAP. At the end of each PTA, questions are posed for the reader to peruse. The final section of this chapter puts forward a summary of the PTA key points.

Note on vocabulary

L. Dyer, *A Humanistic Approach to English for Academic Purposes Pedagogy*,
https://doi.org/10.1007/978-3-032-00186-3_2

This chapter makes use of the terms approach and thought. These two words could be interpreted in multiple ways and could be referred to as theory, ideology, concept, philosophy and framework amongst others. I do not seek to define each of these terms as this is not the focus of this work. But for clarity each of these terms can be considered as referring to an idea that has been developed for use within educational contexts.

2.2 What Is Humanism?

Before embarking on a presentation of a theory on a humanistic approach to EAP, it is important to review exactly what humanism is. Humanism in its various forms, interpretations and applications has existed in multiple cultural philosophical contexts for millennia with its key consideration being for the welfare of human beings (Lamont 1957). In Ancient Greece humanism was explored through various perspectives such as religious doctrines, the development of one's character and the will not to harm another (Law 2011). This can be elucidated as the being of harmony and respect between humans. It is through this specific perspective that the term 'humanism' entered the English language from German in the early nineteenth century as the notion of Western classical study (Iannone 2013). As humanism expanded, it became associated with Christianity and the beliefs that God created humans to promote dignity and welfare following the Christianisation of European cultures (Blackburn 2016). This placed Christianity at the forefront of humanistic thought in Europe. However, during the Renaissance this link to religious connotations was broken down, with humanistic thought then becoming a movement free from religion and focusing on cultural enlightenment (Rahman 2013). Here it became synonymous with the joy of unity between humans and nature. Later, particularly in the twentieth century, it developed into a non-religious movement which focused on self-existence and the human capacity for choice (Blackburn 2016). It is this twentieth century form of humanism which forms the contemporary foundation of secular humanistic learning thought and processes. From these contexts it has been argued that humanism is both a non-philosophy due to its origins in the study of Western literary classicism and a philosophy due to its function as an ideology (Iannone 2013). It is the philosophical perspective that forms the basis of this publication. The philosophical perspective of humanism is one that emphasises, amongst others the importance of creativity, collaboration, empathy and human growth (Iannone 2013). Happiness is a core principle of humanism, with happiness taking many forms such as positivity, self-fulfilment, enjoyment in seeking resolutions to problems (Lamont 1957), dignity and respect for others (Law 2011).

2.3 Defining Humanism

As shown in Sect. 2.2, humanism covers an array of different fields, of which each may have its own definition. As such, providing a clear definition of humanism can prove challenging. Humanism crosses many boundaries such as religion, psychology and education; yet to provide a single clearcut definition for any of these fields is 'impossible' (Cave 2009). This section aims to draw some conclusions on a definition of humanism and education.

As this publication's 'type' of humanism originated in the field of psychology, this is perhaps the most obvious place to begin. A psychological perspective of humanism may take a positive approach, highlighting Maslow's and Rogers' notions of love and growth leading to self-power (Cardwell 2014). Humanism also promotes the uniqueness of the individual through valuing their personal interests and goals. Additionally, psychological humanism proposes that humans are inherently good and have the ability to self-actualise (Corsini 2016). Humanism therefore puts trust in the individual in determining their own routes to accomplishments (Pursewell 2019). Interestingly, a definition for humanistic therapy as an approach to foster growth self-understanding (Collins III and O'Brien, eds. 2011) is particularly useful in understanding what humanism aims to do. This definition focuses on the individual to take responsibility for their actions once they are provided with the right conditions to do so.

However, as this publication is about humanism and education it is also important to consider an educational definition of humanism.

Surprisingly this is more challenging to ascertain as humanism is a term that is not commonly found in education dictionaries. Instead, humanistic approaches such as student-centred learning are found to have their own entries rather than grouped together under the humanism label. Given that humanistic approaches to education may have taken a backseat to or perhaps might not be as developed as other approaches, this is perhaps not unexpected. Based on this, elements from psychological definitions of humanism alongside individually listed humanistic educational entries can be used to develop a definition of humanism and education. A definition of humanism in education can therefore be said to be one in which individual learner interests and aspirations are placed at the forefront of the learning process. Through these actions the learner undertakes a process of self-actualisation to develop their own powers of learning with each of these actions unique to the individual learner.

2.4 A Humanistic Education

Following its departure from religious connotations and promoting of social concepts, it was inevitable that aspects of humanism became embedded into education, starting during the European Renaissance (Grendler 2022). As an ideology, humanism allows for the learner to undertake a journey of self-awareness and make their own choices (Yanita and Sumarni 2024) in order to develop the whole person in the learning process (Prabhavathy and Mahalakshmi 2012). Learners are considered to be individuals who should be viewed as the starting point for the educational journey. In this sense educators would act as facilitators, as opposed to the holder and supplier of knowledge. Thus the educator would instead foster the conditions for a positive learning experience (Wallace 2015). Hence, a humanistic education seeks to nurture as opposed to construct the learner (Rahman 2013). By placing the learner at the centre, the learning experience can become one which cultivates student empowerment and autonomy (Aloni 2013). To promote this personal skills development, teaching methods should be appropriate (Russo 1995) and would cater for learner needs rather than following a prescribed curriculum. This would allow for learners to establish their own responsibilities (Goldstein and Fernald 2010) and be actively involved in the learning process (Wright 2011). This could be achieved through the use of the concept of self-knowledge. The concept of self-knowledge is developed through two sources: intrinsically through reflection and externally through interaction with external sources such as education (Feigenbaum 2024).

As a result of the expansion of humanism through education, the twentieth century saw educational psychologists establish a set of principles for the use of humanism in education. These are:

- Humans carry an intrinsic being of goodness
- Humans have free will
- Humans respect one another
- Self-awareness and self-development are essential

(Meadows 2023)

These principles were further developed to encourage more positive outcomes in education, not only in academic terms but also mentally and socially (Matthews 1991, Moscowitz 1993, Shourini 2010; Weaver and Matthews 1993 all cited in PourAli et al. 2017). The principles propose the following are needed for a humanistic education:

- A positive environment that provides safety, encouragement, respect, responsive and a tolerant learning space.
- Students who are intrinsically motivated to learn without reward or punishment and self-direct their learning.
- Teachers who act as facilitators to promote a positive learning environment and experience who can help to develop the above points.
- Opportunity for a reflective and self-evaluative experience to encourage independent growth and learning.

(PourAli et al. 2017)

Alongside pedagogy, emotions are also important to consider in humanistic educational practices. A learner's emotional state can impact on the learning process and that affective actions should be treated as important as cognition in learner acquisition (Mohammad et al. 2013; Yamita and Sumarni 2024). It is here that perhaps humanism could be referred to as 'humane' as it calls for awareness of sensitivities (Aloni 2013) empathy, emotion and learner involvement in education (Rahman 2013). In a humanistic approach, the learning process and conditions are essential. If these two factors are not considered then cognitive educational processes are declined (Arifi 2017). Successful learning depends on the quality of community and belonging a leaner may feel (Arifi 2017), meaning that if there is a sense of lacking in these areas there is potential for the learner not to achieve their potential.

Whilst humanistic approaches to education may be viewed positively, they may not be applied for a number of reasons. For example, educational institutions may wish to achieve specific measurable goals, such as the number of students achieving 'top grades'. Yet this can be detrimental to other forms of learning and success as using measurable goals can lead to a controlling curriculum (Higgins 2015) where learners are ushered in the direction of 'top grades' at the expense of developing personal skills. Additionally, although student-centred learning (see Sect. 2.6.1.3) has become embedded in many aspects of HE teaching and learning, other humanistic approaches to education are not widely used (PourAli et al. 2017). Instead other approaches in place increase the potential for lower levels of self-esteem, motivation and learning outcomes (Maboubeh et al. 2009; Wenzhong and Youzhong 2006; Matthews 1991 all cited in PourAli et al. 2017).

2.5 Why Would EAP Benefit from a Humanistic Approach?

Although it is noticeable that aspects of humanism have filtered into some segments of EAP (see Jakonen and Duran 2024; Rajendram and Shi 2022; Jin et al. 2022) a more embedded humanistic approach has not materialised. This means that the EAP student must continue to navigate a range of pathways that might be less compassionate to their situation (see Sect. 4.6). Although no student of EAP is a beginner in the English language (see Sect. 4.5), they may still experience negative emotions as they seek to attain linguistic expectations. Learning a new language, or in EAP's case linguistic expectations, reverts the learner back to a language acquisition stage which can place them in a context where they are unable to fully express themselves as they would in their L1. This can generate negative emotions that can impact on the learning process (Stevick 1980). As stated in Chapter 1, EAP aims to prepare students for undertaking academic studies through the English language and it does this by using a standardised set of norms for what is deemed necessary linguistically and skills wise. This lays the foundation for power relations which place educators and EAP providers at the top of the hierarchy perpetuating the set of norms and ideologies of what is necessary for EAP (Hyland 2018). It does not take into account the individual, their pathway through the learning process and how emotions may impact on their journey. One reason for this power structure is potentially financial. EAP is now a valuable asset in the education sector globally. It is a sector of education that can relatively easily be both implemented and removed by providers as they seek to match financial expectations (Hyland 2018; Bruce 2022). Providers seek to offer academic qualifications through the language of English to increase both prestige and finances. The result has been an upsurge in demand for EAP provision. This has led to an increasing number of providers taking a top-down approach to EAP as they endeavour to supply their consumers (Bruce 2022), i.e. the EAP student, with EAP courses (Hyland 2018) with the aim of increasing revenue. However, this may be at the expense of the learning experience as curricula are aligned to frameworks such as CEFR (Bruce 2022) or IELTS (Pearson 2020) rather than catering to what specific student cohorts may benefit from. By using frameworks, there is the potential to see the EAP student as a learner in deficit. For example, a student may not achieve a score that reflects their true speaking capabilities due to the impact of shyness or social-connectedness with their peers (Gao et al. 2022). Because of this and the controlling nature of curricula frameworks, teachers may take control of student learning practice to encourage the development of areas of 'issue'. This may lead to the development of negative emotions from the student which in turn may impact on their learning experience (Tilga et al. 2019). Further controlling student learning practices includes aspects such as:

- repeating skills practice until the learner has got the 'right answer' through a process of pressure
- choosing material content the educator may personally feel the student needs know as citizens but is not directly related to their EAP or disciplinary studies, thus pressuring students to conform and put aside their own opinion
- placing the teacher at the top of the classroom hierarchy as the person with the knowledge and things must be done in the way they dictate

(Reeve 2009)

For those EAP practitioners with some degree of freedom in their teaching it is important to consider what perspective they have of the EAP student, how this may influence their pedagogical practices and the impact this may have on the learner (Thornton and McEntee 2011). These pedagogical practices have the potential to slow down, demotivate or put up barriers to the individual's learning processes (Reeve 2009). Moving away from benchmarked frameworks could provide students with a more fruitful learning experience that evaluates them through multiple means rather than a numbered level of achievement. The use of humanistic practices in EAP courses could change how students learn and develop. These practices can be integrated into teaching and learning in order to reduce and potentially nullify negative feelings students may feel around lack of agency and efficacy. It has the potential to foster conditions of positivity in the learning experience through the restoring of positive processes and emotions (Meadows 2023). Humanism offers the chance to remove the power relations mentioned above and provide a more all-round approach to the EAP student's learning experience. Humanism in language education is not a recent phenomenon, with approaches to learning such as *Suggestopedia*, *SW* and *Community Language Learning* having existed for several decades. Each of these approaches are humanistic in that they focus on the learner rather than linguistic functions (Sharp 2012). Although EAP is not language learning per se, it is a language acquisitor and thus could also make use of humanistic approaches. Humanism can provide a more positive learning outcome for students (Javadi and Tahamsbi 2020) as it is about fitting the learning around the learner as opposed to moulding the learner to a desired outcome. Whilst a humanistic approach to EAP may be considered too 'soft' and not suitable for the EAP learner due to the creative and enjoyable activities, the opportunity for students to learn through that approach could prove beneficial in terms of confidence and self-esteem (Tomlinson 2008).

2.6 PTAs in Humanistic Education

To highlight the successes of humanism in general and language education, this next section looks at PTAs that have had a significant impact on one or both. These PTAs are briefly reviewed with key elements linked to pedagogy highlighted. An explanation of how these PTAs could benefit EAP is included in each section. Each PTA section ends with questions for the practitioner to consider in their practice. Although there are multiple other PTAs that could be considered humanistic or contain elements of humanism (for example feminism and social theory), it is the ones that could be considered most relevant to pedagogy that are included in this chapter. The PTAs reviewed in this section are separated into three groups. The first group consists of the following:

- Montessori's 'Method'
- Maslow's hierarchy of needs
- Rogers' student-centred learning

Each of these could be considered to have had significant longstanding impact on educational practices. They emerged as a result of working directly with education or through transferal from another field to education.

The second group consists of PTAs that contain humanistic elements that can be linked to pedagogy. These PTAs are presented in alphabetical order:

- Affective learning
- Aloni's principles for humanistic pedagogy
- Csikszentmihalyi's theory of flow
- Motivation
- Pekrun's achievement emotions
- Positive education
- Stevick's elements of humanism
- Sustainable learning
- TBL
- Vygotsky's SCT

The final group consists of PTAs specifically for language learning. These PTAs contain aspects of humanistic pedagogy, though some elements may now considered to be unsuitable for contemporary educational practices. These PTAs are:

- Gattegno's SW
- Lozanov's Suggestopedia

2.6.1 Group 1: Montessori, Maslow and Rogers

As aforementioned, this group consists of work that could be considered to have had significant impact on the field of education. Montessori's 'Method' was developed as a direct result of the creator working in education. The works of Maslow and Rogers stem from psychology but were subsequently transferred to education.

2.6.1.1 Montessori's 'Method'

An early prominent example of humanism in education is found in the work of the Italian educator Maria Montessori (1870–1952). Her work with young children developed into an alternative pedagogical approach that has continued to the present day through the worldwide establishment of Montessori schools (Montessori Education (UK) Ltd 2024). These schools educate children through what is now termed the

Montessori Method. Montessori's approach recognised each child as an individual that should have the freedom to choose what to learn. The approach stressed importance on the role of intrinsic motivation in the learning process. It may be asked why Montessori is included in this publication about EAP pedagogy for largely adult education. The reason for her inclusion is that there are two main features of Montessori's work that link strongly with PPCP and as such she could be considered influential in its creation. The first feature is the role of curiosity in learning. In the Montessori Method stimuli are used to gain a child's interest which generates curiosity and potential subsequent intrinsic motivation to learn. The teacher then reacts to the response from the child to guide the learning process, highlighting the teacher's role as one of a facilitator (Giardiello 2014). The role of curiosity has featured in works of others, notably Paulo Freire who argued that curiosity was an innate characteristic of all humans. It is through curiosity we can develop epistemologically (Lewis 2012) and because of epistemology that we are curious (Leistyna 2004). The second relevant feature of Montessori's work is the importance of the learning environment. She adapted classrooms to suit the needs of young learners such as through lightweight furniture that a child could carry as opposed to heavy fixed desks and chairs found in the traditional classroom setting (Montessori 1965 cited in Giardiello 2014). Although Montessori's approach was designed for the education of young children, both curiosity and consideration for the learning environment could also be applied to older learners. High levels of curiosity have been shown to enhance learning through intrinsic motivation (Gruber et al. 2014). Through the use of tasks that increase curiosity, the learner can have the opportunity for a more successful learning outcome. This aspect of the Montessori Method could prove beneficial in EAP by increasing interest and challenge for the learner through activities that arouse curiosity. Tasks that encourage exploration, experimentation and sensory activities (Montessori Teachers Training 2025) can be used as an opportunity to experience student-centred learning (see Sect. 2.6.1.3) and increase intrinsic motivation (see Sect. 2.6.2.4). In terms of the learning environment, the physicality of the classroom too has the potential to impact on the learning experience and higher learning performances (Jamaludin et al. 2016). It could also be applied to teaching techniques within the learning environment such as flipped classrooms (Fernández-Moya et al. 2020). As will be demonstrated through the presentation of PPCP in Chapter 5, the role of the environment or place is essential in determining the success of a pedagogical activity. If an environment is less suitable for an activity, it will become more challenging to achieve a successful outcome. For the EAP student who is navigating an array of pathways in their EAP learning process (see Chapter 4), a benefitting learning environment could prove a positive constituent in their journey.

Reflective questions on Montessori's Method

- How could curiosity be integrated into EAP learning activities?
- How can the learning environment be set up to provide a positive learning experience? Can the learning environment be adapted according to the pedagogical activity?

2.6.1.2 Maslow's Hierarchy of Needs

Psychologist Abraham Maslow (1908–1970) developed the hierarchy of needs as a model to represent what is considered to be the scale of human needs (Rojas et al. 2023). This pyramidal model consists of five categories of needs which are attained through progression from the foundation to the peak. The five categories starting from the foundation are:

- Biological and psychological needs—the basic needs for life such as food and water
- Safety needs—stability, protection and integrity
- Belonging and love needs—family, friendship and companionship
- Esteem needs—self-worth, confidence, achievement and reputation
- Self-actualisation—achieving one's full potential

(Maslow 1943 and 1954 cited in Rojas et al. 2023)

Experience and creativity are the two key principles behind Maslow's humanistic psychology ideology in a successful educational process which he applied these to his own teaching practices (Feigenbaum

2024). Through these principles Maslow promoted the need for intrinsic learning and 'peak experiences' in order for learners to have a successful learning experience (Feigenbaum 2024). Maslow (1962) describes a peak experience as one of positivity and happiness where all ruminations and negative distractions are lost. These can occur in any person though they may not be recognised every individual as a peak experience. Peak experiences also have the potential to change a person's outlook (Maslow 1962). This could perhaps be best described as a lightbulb moment and is part of the hierarchy of needs' esteem needs as the learner gains confidence and self-worth on their pathway to self-actualisation. However, Maslow argued that much of education was designed to 'please the teacher' (Feigenbaum 2024) instead of encouraging creativity essential for the peak experience. The result of this is that learners have less chance of achieving self-actualisation. Although Maslow placed labels on the five categories, these are subjective and the individual may feel satisfaction with any of the levels in the hierarchy. For example, a student may feel satisfaction in achieving a high grade in an assessment. This may be the pinnacle of the student's achievement with this activity; they may choose not to progress to self-actualisation yet still remain satisfied. The notion of progression may also be question as a learner may move up or down the hierarchy which could be as a result of internal or external drivers (see Sect. 4.6).

A humanistic educational approach can use Maslow's principles in providing a learning experience that provides the learner with opportunities for creativity, independence and positivity. For EAP, this could be a diversion away from the mechanistic approaches to learning can allow creative processes to take place. Allowing students to undertake more creative practices could enable them to progress through the levels of the hierarchy of needs.

Reflective questions on Maslow's hierarchy of needs

- Where are EAP students currently situated on the hierarchy of needs?
- How could EAP students progress to the next category on the hierarchy of needs?

2.6.1.3 Rogers' Student-Centred Learning

Carl Rogers (1902–1987) is credited with being amongst the instigators of the concept of human potential. Human potential stresses the human's ability to take control of their circumstances through processes of self-reflection and actualisation (Burgan and Congos 2008). Through this, Rogers developed a humanistic approach to pedagogical practice through the concept of student-centeredness (Rogers 1967, 1968 cited in Feigenbaum 2024). Rogers' student-centred approach establishes the teacher as a person of support rather than a communicator of knowledge (Rahman 2013). It takes away the teacher from being the source of authority who tells students what they should know. Instead the student-centred approach highlights the teacher's role in the building of learner confidence and self-esteem through a teacher-student partnership in decision making. The teacher becomes the facilitator, providing students with a context in which they learn how to learn is one that has the most potential to support learning (Rogers 2001). The facilitator cares for the individual learner in their individual educational journey, is aware of and supports the learner through their negative and positive educational experiences (Rogers 2001). As with Montessori, Rogers advocates for the promotion of curiosity in the learning process, where learners are enthused by carrying out work guided by their own interests which in turn opens up new avenues of learning (Rogers 2001). As such student-centred learning emphasises the importance of both intellectual and emotional discovery as a means to a positive learning experience (Feigenbaum 2024). For EAP, a student-centred approach could replicate the independent learning expected to take place during academic studies, where students make their own judgements and decisions rather than relying solely on the teacher.

Reflective questions on Rogers' student-centred learning

- What is the role of the EAP practitioner in the learning process?
- What pedagogical activities could benefit from a student-centred approach?

2.6.1.4 Humanistic Learning Theory

Together with Maslow and James F.T. Bugental, Rogers put forward humanistic learning theory which outline tenets of a humanistic education needed to achieve self-actualisation. These tenets are:

- Student-centred learning—respecting and allowing student choice in their educational journey.
- Fostering student engagement—developing a context in which students become motivated to learn.
- Self-reflection—moving away from a top-down approach to assessment to one in which the student evaluates how they feel about their learning. A top-down approach to assessment may not be a meaningful indicator of learning, instead students should be trusted to reflect on their own progress (Stommel 2024).
- The importance of emotion in knowledge generation—pedagogy should reflect both knowledge and emotions in the learning process.
- A protective learning environment—one in which the learner feels they are able to learn as well as one in they feel safe mentally, emotionally and physically.

(Western Governors University 2020)

Existing approaches to EAP may allow for some of these tenets to be applied. However, as shown in Chapter 3, contexts may not allow for the administration of all aspects of humanistic learning theory. Nevertheless, an increased awareness of these tenets may prove beneficial to EAP pedagogical design, no matter how light touch they may be.

2.6.2 Group 2: Affective Learning, Aloni, Csiszentmihalyi, Motivation, Pekrun, Positive Education, Stevick, Sustainable Learning, TBL and Vygotsky

This next group of PTAs use humanistic principles that have been designed for or could be used in pedagogical situations. These PTAs are presented in alphabetical order according to the architect's name. Where there is no specific named author, the PTA is placed according to its name.

2.6.2.1 Affective Learning

Affective learning proposes that emotions play a role in defining a learner's educational success. For example, negative emotions may hinder a student's progress but positive emotions can increase intrinsic motivation levels (Derakhshan et al. 2023) and potentially ensuing successful outcomes. Affective learning advocates that learners obtain knowledge and skills through emotional engagement (Mahadeo and Nepal 2023). The affect a learner experiences can subsequently impact on the interaction with stimuli (Gläser-Zikuda 2012). Factors which can influence the affect include content, assessment type and the teacher (Derakhshan et al. 2023). For example, situations which the student may consider as high stakes may produce negative emotions such as stress and anxiety (Cahour 2013). Removing or reducing the potential for these negative emotions places the student in a context where a more positive outcome is possible. As EAP is the gatekeeper for many students wishing to undertake academic studies, negative emotions could come to the fore as learners strive to achieve designated achievement levels (Payant et al. 2019). Providing students with an environment that minimises the potentiality of unfavourable outcomes could help to lower the impact of negative affects. By considering and lessening aspects of pedagogical activities have the potential to cause negative emotions, EAP can provide learners with more opportunities to succeed.

Reflective questions on affective learning

- What EAP pedagogical activities may cause negative emotions?
- How can negative emotions be reduced or removed from pedagogical activities?

2.6.2.2 Aloni's Principles of Humanistic Pedagogy

A central figure in contemporary humanistic education is Nimrod Aloni. For Aloni humanistic education promotes the removal of intellectual suppression through autonomy, creativity and valuing the individual (Aloni 2011). His work splits humanistic educational practices into two parts. Firstly the teaching of humanistic content and secondly the use of humanistic approaches in educational practice. Through this second aspect, sets of principles and characteristics for humanistic education were developed. The key principles proposed by Aloni for humanistic pedagogy are:

- Acculturation—how one adapts and integrates into a culture (Aloni 1997).
- Autonomy—the role of self-determination how a learner undertakes their studies (Aloni 1997).
- Authenticity—how the learner portrays themselves in their learning such as through voice (Aloni 1997). Authenticity also impacts on the practice of the educator who should provide opportunities for the learner to be authentic. This in turn can lead to increased engagement from the learner (Henry and Thorsen 2018).

Furthermore, for educational practice to be considered as humanistic, it should contain the following:

- Opportunities for the student to foster and develop their learning
- Positive interpersonal relations promoting respect and kindness
- Trust and acceptance of others and differences
- An environment that encourages knowledge and expertise
- Meaningful teaching methods

(Aloni 2013)

Reflective questions on Aloni's principles of humanistic pedagogy

- How does EAP enable academic acculturation?
- How much autonomy does an EAP learner have?

- What role does authenticity play in the EAP classroom?

2.6.2.3 Csikszentmihalyi's Theory of Flow

Developed into a theory by Mihalyi Csikszentmihalyi, flow is the positive psychological state where the human is fully engaged and focused on a task (Beard 2015). This state of being 'in the zone' is characterised by intense concentration, the disappearance of anxieties and ruminations, a heightened sense of control, temporal distortions and high levels of intrinsic motivation and satisfaction over the task (Keller et al. 2011). This surmises that the ideal conditions for peak learning are those in which the student feels fully engaged and motivated in pedagogical tasks, in which they are able to concentrate entirely on the task in hand to such an extent that negative states and emotions are banished. As mentioned earlier, EAP often uses mechanistic approaches to teaching and learning. Providing a different learning experience has the potential to increase levels of curiosity, intrinsic motivation and the chance to be 'in the zone'.

Reflective questions on Csikszentmihalyi's theory of flow

- How could flow be encouraged in EAP pedagogical activities?

2.6.2.4 Motivation

Motivation can be defined as the choice to engage in an action, persist with it and how much effort to put in (Dörnyei and Ushioda 2021). Zoltan Dörnyei and Ema Ushioda's work on motivation and language learning takes on aspects of humanism in its approach. Their framework for motivational strategies encompasses four elements:

1. Creating positive and supportive learning conditions. This should be both in the physical learning environment and through peer to peer and peer to teacher interpersonal relationships
2. Generating learner motivation through authentic and relevant activities

3. Maintaining motivation through providing a clear task structure giving students ownership of its processes and outcomes
4. Encouraging a positive self-reflection upon completion of the task

Providing learning conditions with these four elements increases the chance of learning motivation to occur.

Dörnyei also proposed that motivation in language learning can be attributed to the concept of the future self (2005, cited Dörnyei 2009), in which the future self consists of the 'ideal' and 'ought to' self. The ideal self describes how the learner would envisage themselves as a successful language learner and is controlled by intrinsic processes. The ought to self is determined more extrinsically than the ideal self and illustrates what the student feels they should be achieving (Dörnyei 2005 cited in Dörnyei 2009; Papi and Abdollahzadeh 2012). As the ought to self contains elements of extrinsic motivation, there is the possibility for more negative emotions in the learning process which could impact on its outcomes (Papi 2010). The ought to self may result in the learner comparing themselves to standards or peers which takes them away from individual learning processes. In contrast, the positive ideal self is determined by the individual and self-imagery. It has been shown that being self-motivated can strengthen the desire to succeed and that this can encourage successful learning (Anwar and Wardhono 2019). These self-generated humanistic thought processes can be harnessed by educators as the basis for Dörnyei and Ushioda's (2021) motivational framework strategy to create positive learning experiences. As a preparator or supporter of academic studies through the medium of English, EAP has the opportunity for learners to visualise an ideal self undertaking disciplinary work through the English language.

Reflective questions on motivation

- How can learners experience the ideal self in their EAP studies?

2.6.2.5 Pekrun's Achievement Emotions

Reinhard Pekrun's work on achievement emotions can also be considered as a humanistic approach through the development of a learner's positive psychology. The term achievement emotion is directly related to achievements made in activities and consequently in their outcomes (Pekrun 2006). A positive achievement emotion during activities does not necessarily lead to positive achievement emotion in outcomes. Conversely the same can apply to negative achievement emotions. However, experiencing positive achievement emotions is more likely to result in positive outcomes. In order to foster the conditions for positive achievement emotions, Pekrun (2006) proposes the following factors:

- Pitching tasks at a level that is neither too challenging nor too easy for the learner
- Tasks that meet the need of the students, such as authentic tasks and engage all learners
- Develop a learning environment that facilitates learner autonomy and co-operation between peers
- Avoiding excessive amounts of failure feedback, instead focusing on the positives and suggested areas for learning

Reflective questions on Pekrun's achievement emotions

- How can positivity be encouraged in the EAP classroom?
- How can authenticity be built into pedagogical activities?
- How can tasks develop learner autonomy?

2.6.2.6 Positive Education

Positive education is based on the principle that by taking care of a learner's emotional well-being they will have the opportunity for greater learning success (Cabanas and González-Lamas 2022). Educational success is traditionally measured by academic achievement but there has been growing interest in evaluating other outcomes such as mindset and well-being (Arguís-Rey 2021). It is noticeable that this forms part of OECD's (2017) Programme for Student Assessment and is supported by Rogers' work on the emotional mindset of the student in achieving desired outcomes (see Sect. 2.6.1.3 learning). Thus positive education is recognised as being significant in global education. Already in use across a variety of educational levels in Australia (White and Kern 2018; Slemp et al. 2017; Seligman et al. 2009), positive education consists of two elements:

1. The teaching of 'positivity' content
2. Adaption and creation of activities that promote a positive psychology

For the purposes of this chapter it is the second aspect, activities designed to promote a positive psychology, that form the majority part of humanistic approach to pedagogical design in EAP. A humanistic approach to education can be considered a positive educational experience that places the learner first through the development of a positive psychology (Slemp et al. 2017). Positive education focuses on a range of aspects such as happiness, engagement, psychosocial skills, emotional resilience, autonomy and intrinsic motivation, with many of these highlighted as components of humanistic educational thought. A positive education celebrates strengths, optimism and a positive mindset (Arguís-Rey 2021) and distances negative states (Ciarrochi et al. 2016). As such developing the learner as a whole, such as through increasing learner confidence, is just as important as learning knowledge. EAP may particularly benefit from positive education approaches as students enter what could be seen as an 'alien' learning environment. As stated in Chapter 4, the EAP student is often viewed as being in deficit. Changing this deficit opinion to one of difference could provide a more positive educational experience for the EAP student.

Reflective questions on positive education

- To what extent does EAP view the student as being in deficit?
- Could aspects of deficit be changed to difference?
- What activities could encourage positive education in EAP?

2.6.2.7 Stevick's Elements of Humanism

Earl W. Stevick was an advocate of humanistic approaches to education and its application to language learning (Humanising Language Teaching, n.d.). His work with humanistic approaches was initially applied to his own teaching practices before being disseminated through publications to encourage teachers to have a better understanding of their own work (Stevick 2000). For teaching practice to be considered as humanistic, pedagogies should take into account the following elements:

- Emotion
- Social relations
- Responsibility
- Intellectual development
- Self-actualisation

(Stevick 1990)

As stated earlier, EAP may take on a hierarchical power structure which places the learner at the bottom (see Sect. 2.5). For Stevick's elements of humanism to be achieved, this construct should be altered to place the learner at a different level, or ideally the top, of the pyramid.

Reflective questions on Stevick's elements of humanism

- How do EAP teachers reflect on their own teaching practices?
- How can an EAP teacher reduce hierarchical classroom structures?

2.6.2.8 Sustainable Learning

The concept of sustainable learning is twofold. Firstly it is the teaching of content that concerns responsible practices in the area of sustainability. That is to say it provides learners with the skills and knowledge for supporting a sustainable ecosystem in the literal sense (Kinchin 2024). Secondly it is the practice of providing students with purposeful, proactive, ongoing skills and knowledge that can be retained (Hays and Reinders 2020). This could perhaps be considered a sustainable ecosystem in the figurative sense (Kinchin 2024). Sustainable learning is one which has a long-term meaningful impact on the learner as an individual (Van den Branden 2012). It can be both a formal and informal process and should have aspects of self-sufficiency embedded into it (Hays and Reinders 2020). For a learning process to be sustainable, it should focus on transitions in educational settings, including moving between different educational stages and eventual progression beyond education (Graham et al. 2015). According to sustainable learning principles, a sustainable learning experience will provide learners with the skills and attributes to succeed and be proactive in a range of changing and challenging contexts. This is because a sustainable learning experience is not one that solely focuses on the accumulation of knowledge but also the skills and capabilities to succeed in a learning environment (Hays and Reinders 2020). Sustainable learning could be seen as a humanistic approach to education in that it considers the development of the individual as a whole. As shown in Sect. 1.3, EAP usually consists of developing a learner's linguistic and academic skills. Should community skills be included in EAP, there is potential for sustainable learning.

Reflective questions on sustainable learning

- Can EAP support the development of community skills?
- Can EAP support the learner beyond their EAP study?

2.6.2.9 TBL

TBL is an approach where learners undertake a task that does not have strongly defined linguistic outcomes, rather success in the task is determined by its completion. The task may be based around a topic of choice, meaning that there is opportunity for learners to have input on the tasks they undertake such as with the content or the type of activity. TBL can be considered humanistic in that it discourages teacher input and instead places the learner at the centre as they carry out tasks. Tasks can be carried out in groups or individually, but the key feature of this is that there are opportunities for the use of English (Viriya 2018) which is carried out in an authentic context (Xu 2021). In order for a task to be considered authentic it should be one that could take place in academic studies such as seminars (see Basturkmen 2002) or academic reading circles (see Xu 2021). In EAP TBL can provide opportunity to carry out tasks that are linked content wise to student's academic studies whilst also developing the necessary academic skills and linguistic capabilities (see Sect. 1.3). TBL is a chance to put language and skills into practice with success judged on the completion of the task.

Reflective questions on TBL

- What authentic TBL tasks could be used in EAP pedagogies?

2.6.2.10 Vygotsky's SCT

Developed by Lev Vygotsky (1896–1934), SCT was initially applied to how individual learners acquire knowledge and skills through interaction with society and culture. Subsequently it has been comprehensively applied in the field of applied linguistics and second language acquisition (Swain et al. 2015, see Poehner et al. 2018). SCT proposes that humans learn from interaction with each other such as through noticing or sharing (Lantolf et al. 2018). Although SCT focused on human learning as a whole, there was a push from the L2 community to consider its role in language acquisition. This resulted in the application of SCT to aid language learning (Lantolf et al. 2018). A range of pedagogies have developed in second language acquisition as a result of SCT (van Compernolle and Williams 2013). Examples of pedagogic tasks developed in this way include the teacher providing learners with a task-based learning activity, promoting the use of technology to enhance the learning experience (van Compernolle and Williams 2013), games (Lantolf and Poehner 2023) as well as learning from others through activities such as a language exchange. In these activities it can be seen that the teacher has a role as mediator or facilitator in language learning and that the learner takes control of their learning. As the acquisition of language progresses, the learners become less reliant on external influence and instead develop internalised dialogue in which they guide themselves through the learning process (Lantolf and Poehner 2023). As the majority of EAP takes place in tertiary education (see Sect. 3.3.1), learners at this level are expected to have a greater degree of autonomy and self-directed learning (Wilson et al. 2017). Thus there is potential for SCT to occur.

A further aspect of SCT is the concept of ZPD. The ZPD separates levels human development into three categories:

- What is known
- What can be learnt through collaboration with another person
- What is not known

(Eun 2017)

This separation acknowledges the existence of what is already known. This aspect can be said to be lacking in EAP as it often takes a deficit approach to teaching and learning. Acknowledging the learner's existing skills and knowledge could 'speed up' the EAP learning process by focusing on the unknown and what can be learnt rather than repeating or reviewing what a student is already aware of. This is reflected in compendium activity 6.5.

Reflective questions on Vygotsky's SCT

- Can technology, games or language exchange aid EAP study?
- How can the EAP student's existing knowledge and skills help them in their EAP learning?

2.6.3 Group 3: Gattegno and Lozanov

As one function of EAP is to develop linguistic skills for academic studies (see Sect. 1.3), it is useful to also look at humanistic approaches that have been specifically applied or developed for language teaching. Although they may take a backseat to more recent ideologies (Harmer 2021), these methods demonstrate that the use of humanistic approaches have been applied to language teaching over a significant period of time. These methods are SW and Suggestopedia. Due to the age of these methods, certain aspects may be considered outdated or inappropriate for contemporary educational practices. Additionally, as they were not specifically designed for EAP they are not tailored to the needs of the EAP. However, there are elements of these methods that can still be applied to the EAP context and these are highlighted.

2.6.3.1 Gattegno's SW

SW, created by Caleb Gattegno, can be considered a humanistic approach due to the role of the teacher in the learning process. In the SW, the teacher moves from a central figure of authority in the classroom to one of a facilitator and observer. A SW teacher's vocalisations are kept to a minimum in order to allow for learners to discover and create more language (Harmer 2021). Through this a student can gain more independence, agency and self-responsibility for their learning (Rahman 2013). Student errors are not corrected by the teacher but can be corrected by peers (Rahman 2013). For EAP, the SW can raise awareness of the teaching style learners may experience in their academic studies where learner proactivity may be expected.

Reflective questions on SW

- How much does the teacher need to speak in the EAP classroom?
- Are EAP students able to correct peer errors?

2.6.3.2 Lozanov's Suggestopedia

In the 1970s Georgi Lozanov proposed that barriers to learning can increase stress levels and anxiety which can impact on outcomes. Through this he developed Suggestopedia which aims to quell negative feelings (Harmer 2021) can impact on capability and potentiality. Suggestopedia consists of several components, of which some may not be considered applicable to EAP contexts (see Garry 1978 for an account of a demonstration of Suggestopedia). Yet there are aspects of Suggestopedia which can be applied to EAP, such as the function of the learning environment. In Suggestopedia the physical surroundings and atmosphere are considered essential factors in the learning experience. As such positivity is reinforced with errors ignored to maintain calmness. The learning environment is carefully constructed to create a conducive and relaxing learning space (Rahman 2013), such as through layout or lighting. In EAP, the learning environment should be suitable for intended pedagogic tasks, such as ensuring Wi-Fi access if in class research is needed or providing user-friendly digital platforms for online learners.

Reflective questions on Suggestopedia

- How can the learning environment aid EAP study?

2.7 Summary of Key Points

As shown above, a humanistic educational approach has many facets. Although there are many PTAs presented in this chapter, there are overlaps with their focus. For example, both the Montessori Method and Suggestopedia place importance on the learning environment. Both the SW and student-centred learning remove the teacher from the learning focal point. Additionally, motivation could be considered as an instance of flow and being in the zone for learning. Despite the differences and similarities, there are overarching elements that should be in place for an educational experience to be considered humanistic. As will be shown later in this publication (see Chapter 4), the EAP student may undergo a different journey to non-EAP students and as such could benefit greatly from a humanistic approach. When creating pedagogical tasks for EAP, the practitioner could take into account any or all of the following to allow for a humanistic learning experience:

- Create a learning experience that focuses on the positive, with negatives kept to a minimum. This can, for example, take the form of materials content, feedback or the suitability of activities for individual learners

- Pedagogical activities should be used as scaffolding tasks to enable the learner to develop the language and skills to enable an internalised self which directs and controls learner processes
- Approaches to pedagogy should be student-centred, allowing for learners to take control of the learning process
- Engage with learner interests to arouse curiosity
- Produce tasks in which the learner can feel engaged and motivated. These tasks should be authentic and be valued by the learner but not repeated in order to avoid the loss of flow
- Create opportunities for peer collaboration to develop language
- Allow opportunities to develop the learner as a whole person alongside their cognition and knowledge acquisition

References

Aloni, Nimrod. 1997. A redefinition of liberal and humanistic education. *International Review of Education* 43: 87–107. https://doi.org/10.1023/A:1002962614704.

Aloni, Nimrod. 2011. Humanistic education. In *Education and humanism. Moral development and citizenship education*, ed. Wiel Veugelers, 35–46. Rotterdam: SensePublishers. https://doi.org/10.1007/978-94-6091-577-2_3.

Aloni, Nimrod. 2013. Empowering dialogues in humanistic education. *Educational Philosophy and Theory* 45 (10): 1067–1081. https://doi.org/10.1111/j.1469-5812.2011.00789.x.

Anwar, Khoirul, and Agus Wardhono. 2019. Students' perception of learning experience and achievement motivation: Prototyping English for academic purposes (EAP). *International journal of instruction* 12 (3): 271–288. https://files.eric.ed.gov/fulltext/EJ1220216.pdf.

Arguís-Rey, Ricardo. 2021. Positive education in practice. In *The Palgrave book of positive education*, ed. Margaret L. Kern and Michael L. Wehmeyer, 49–74. Cham: Palgrave MacMillan.

Arifi, Qatip. 2017. Humanistic approach in teaching foreign languages (from the teacher perspective). *European Scientific Journal* 13 (35): 194–205. https://doi.org/10.19044/esj.2017.v13n35p194.

Basturkmen, Helen. 2002. Negotiating meaning in seminar-type discussion and EAP. *English for Specific Purposes* 21 (3): 233–242. https://doi.org/10.1016/S0889-4906(01)00024-2.

Beard, Karen Stansberry. 2015. Theoretically speaking: An interview with Mihaly Csikszentmihalyi on Flow Theory development and its usefulness in addressing contemporary challenges in education. *Educational Psychological Review* 27: 353–364. https://doi.org/10.1007/s10648-014-9291-1.

Blackburn, Simon. 2016. *The Oxford dictionary of philosophy*, 2nd ed. Oxford: Oxford University Press.

Bruce, Ian. 2022. Universities in the twenty-first century: Structures, funding, management and governance. In *Contextualizing English for academic purposes in higher education: Politics, policies and practices*, ed. Ian Bruce and Bee Bond, 7–26. London: Bloomsbury. https://www.perlego.com/book/3544095.

Burgan, W. Michael, and Dennis H. Congos. 2008. The student-centered SI leader and Carl Rogers. *Research and Teaching in Developmental Education* 25 (1): 3–9. http://www.jstor.org/stable/42802316.

Cabanas, Edgar, and Jara González-Lamas. 2022. A critical review of positive education: Challenges and limitations. *Social Psychology of Education* 25: 1249–1272. https://doi.org/10.1007/s11218-022-09721-7.

Cahour, Béatrice. 2013. Emotions: Characteristics, emergence and circulation in interractional learning. In *Affective learning together: Social and emotional dimensions of collaborative learning*, ed. Michael Baker, Jerry Andriessen, and Sanna Järvelä, 52–70. London: Taylor and Francis.

Cardwell, Mike. 2014. *Dictionary of psychology*. New York: Routledge.

Cave, Peter. 2009. *Humanism for beginners*. Oxford: Oneworld Publications.

Ciarrochi, Joseph, Paul W.B. Atkins, Louise L. Hayes, Baljinder K. Sahdra, and Philip Parker. 2016. Contextual positive psychology: Policy recommendations for implementing positive psychology into schools. *Frontiers in Psychology* 7: 1561. https://doi.org/10.3389/fpsyg.2016.01561.

Collins III, John W., and Nancy Patricia O'Brien. 2011. *The Greenwood dictionary of education*, 2nd ed. Santa Barbara: Greenwood.

Corsini, Ray. 2016. *The dictionary of psychology*. New York: Routledge.

Derakhshan, Ali, Laurence Jun Zhang, and Kiyana Zhaleh. 2023. The effects of instructor clarity and non-verbal immediacy on Chinese and Iranian EFL students' affective learning: The mediating role of instructor understanding. *Studies in Second Language Learning and Teaching* 13 (1): 71–100. https://files.eric.ed.gov/fulltext/EJ1388544.pdf.

Dörnyei, Zoltán. 2009. The L2 motivational self system. In *Motivation, language identity and the L2 self*, ed. Zoltán Dörnyei and Ema Ushioda, 9–42. Bristol: Multilingual Matters.

Dörnyei, Zoltán, and Ema Ushioda. 2021. *Teaching and researching motivation*, 3rd ed. New York, NY: Routledge. https://doi.org/10.4324/9781351006743.

Eun, Barohny. 2017. The zone of proximal development as an overarching concept: A framework for synthesizing Vygotsky's theories. *Educational Philosophy and Theory* 51 (1): 18–30. https://doi.org/10.1080/00131857.2017.1421941.

Feigenbaum, Kenneth D. 2024. A critique of Abraham Maslow and Carl Rogers as educators. *Journal of Humanistic Psychology* 64 (1): 44–63. https://doi.org/10.1177/00221678231154819.

Fernández-Moya, Maria, Pedro Jesús Cuadros, Carlos Salvador, and Jesús María Pinar Pérez. 2020. The Montessori Method in university teaching. INTED2020 Proceedings, 3861–3864. https://doi.org/10.21125/inted.2020.1079.

Gao, Yujie, Wenxian Zhang, Qiuyue Deng, Changlin Sun, Fengqiang Gao, and Yingmin Chen. 2022. Shyness and social adjustment in Chinese college students: A moderated mediation of alienation and school connectedness. *Current Psychology* 41: 1006–1014. https://doi.org/10.1007/s12144-020-01073-9.

Garry, William. W. 1978. Suggestopedia: A new training technique. *Educational Technology* 18 (6): 5–8. http://www.jstor.org/stable/44418997.

Giardiello, Patricia. 2014. *Pioneers in early childhood education the roots and legacies of Rachel and Margaret McMillan, Maria Montessori and Susan Isaacs.* New York: Routledge.

Gläser-Zikuda, Michaela. 2012. Affective and emotional dispositions of/for learning. In *Encyclopedia of the sciences of learning,* ed. Norbert M. Seel, 165–169. Boston, MA: Springer. https://doi.org/10.1007/978-1-4419-1428-6_819.

Goldstein, Gary, and Peter Fernald. 2010. Humanistic education in a capstone course. *College Teaching* 57 (1): 27–36. https://doi.org/10.3200/CTCH.57.1.27-36.

Graham, Lorraine, Jenette Berman, and Anne Bellert. 2015. *Sustainable learning: Inclusive practices for 21st century classrooms.* Cambridge: Cambridge University Press.

Grendler, Paul F. 2022. *Humanism, universities and Jesuit education in late Renaissance Italy.* Boston/Leiden: Brill.

Gruber, Matthias J., Bernard D. Gelman, and Charan Ranganath. 2014. States of curiosity modulate hippocampus-dependent learning via the dopaminergic circuit. *Neuron* 84 (2): 486–496. https://doi.org/10.1016/j.neuron.2014.08.060.

Harmer, Jeremy. 2021. *The practice of English language teaching*, 5th ed. Harlow, Essex: Pearson Education Limited.

Hays, Jay, and Hayo Reinders. 2020. Sustainable learning and education: A curriculum for the future. *International Review of Education* 66: 29–52. https://doi.org/10.1007/s11159-020-09820-7.

Henry, Alastair, and Cecilia Thorsen. 2018. Disaffection and agentic engagement: 'Redesigning' activities to enable authentic self-expression. *Language Teaching Research* 24 (4): 456–475. https://doi.org/10.1177/1362168818795976.

Higgins, Chris. 2015. Humane education. *Educational Theory* 65 (6): 611–615. https://doi.org/10.1111/edth.12137.

Humanizing Language Teaching. n.d. Earl W. Stevick. https://hlt.digital/profiles/earl-w-stevick/. Accessed 4 March 2025.

Hyland, Ken. 2018. Sympathy for the devil? A defence of EAP. *Language Teaching* 51 (3): 383–399. https://doi.org/10.1017/S0261444818000101.

Iannone, A. Pablo. 2013. *Dictionary of world philosophy*. Taylor & Francis.

Jakonen, Teppo, and Derya Duran. 2024. Learner-centered EAP practices: Managing agenda in tutorial interaction. *Journal of English for Academic Purposes* 68: 101345. https://doi.org/10.1016/j.jeap.2024.101345.

Jamaludin, Nurul Malina, Norhayati Mahyuddin, and Farid Wajdi Akashah. 2016. Assessment of indoor environmental quality (IEQ): Students well-being in university classroom with the application of landscaping. *MATEC Web of Conferences* 66: 00061. https://www.matec-conferences.org/articles/matecconf/pdf/2016/29/matecconf_ibcc2016_00061.pdf.

Javadi, Yaghoob, and Mozhdeh Tahamsbi. 2020. Application of humanism teaching theory and humanistic approach to education in coursebooks. *Theory and Practice in Language Studies* 10 (1): 40–48. https://doi.org/10.17507/tpls.1001.06.

Jin, Tan, Yishi Jiang, Michelle Mingyue Gu, and Jing Chen. 2022. "Their encouragement makes me feel more confident": Exploring peer effects on learner engagement on collaborative reading of academic texts. *Journal of English for Academic Purposes* 60: 101177. https://doi.org/10.1016/j.jeap.2022.101177.

Keller, Johannes, Herbert Bless, Frederik Blomann, and Dieter Kleinböhl. 2011. Physiological aspects of flow experiences: Skills-demand-compatibility effects on heart rate variability and salivary cortisol. *Journal of Experimental Social Psychology* 47 (4): 849–852. https://doi.org/10.1016/j.jesp.2011.02.004.

Kinchin, Ian M. 2024. *How to mend a university: Towards a sustainable learning environment in higher education.* London: Bloomsbury.

Lamont, Corliss. 1957. *The philosophy of humanism.* New York: Philosophical Library.

Lantolf, James P., and Matthew E. Poehner. 2023. Sociocultural theory and classroom second language learning in the East Asian context: Introduction to the special issue. *The Modern Language Journal* 107 (S1): 3–23. https://doi.org/10.1111/modl.12816.

Lantolf, James P., Matthew E. Poehner, and Merrill Swain. 2018. Introduction. In *The Routledge handbook of sociocultural theory and second language development*, ed. James P. Lantolf, Matthew E. Poehner, and Merrill Swain, 1–20. Boca Raton, FL: Routledge.

Law, Stephen. 2011. *Humanism: A very short introduction.* Oxford: Oxford University Press.

Leistyna, Pepi. 2004. Presence of mind in the process of learning and knowing: A dialogue with Paulo Freire. *Teacher Education Quarterly* 31 (1): 17–29. https://www.jstor.org/stable/23478410.

Lewis, Tyson S. 2012. Teaching with pensive images: Rethinking Paulo Freire's Pedagogy of the Oppressed. *Journal of Aesthetic Education* 46 (1): 27–45. https://web.s.ebscohost.com/ehost/detail/detail?vid=1&sid=f1390359-f003-4df8-b87d-a3bbef7c8da0%40redis&bdata=JnNpdGU9ZWhvc3QtbG l2ZQ%3d%3d#db=aft&AN=83116178.

Mahadeo, Jyoti Devi, and Rabindra Nepal. 2023. What is affective learning and how can it foster engagement and critical thinking? *Times Higher Education*, 29 September. https://www.timeshighereducation.com/campus/what-affective-learning-and-how-can-it-foster-engagement-and-critical-thinking.

Maslow, Abraham H. 1962. Lessons from the peak-experiences. *Journal of Humanistic Psychology* 2 (1): 9–18. https://doi.org/10.1177/002216786200200102.

Meadows, Bryan. 2023. Humanism in English language teaching. In *Teaching English in global contexts: Language, learners and learning*, ed. Valentina Canese and Susan Spezzini, 69–76. Editorial Facultad de Filosofia, UNA. https://doi.org/10.47133/tegc_ch04.

Mohammad, Khatib, Saeid Sarem, and Hadi Hamidi. 2013. Humanistic education: Concerns, implications and applications. *Journal of Language Teaching and Research* 4 (1): 45–51. https://www.researchgate.net/publication/272797519_Humanistic_Education_Concerns_Implications_and_Applications.

Montessori Education (UK) Ltd. 2024. Montessori method. https://montessorieducationuk.org/. Accessed 12 March 2024.

Montessori Teachers Training. 2025. Nurturing curiosity: Exciting Montessori activities for young minds. https://montessoriteachertraining.org/education/montessori-articles-education/nurturing-curiosity-exciting-montessori-activities-for-young-minds/12198668/. Accessed 26 February 2025.

OECD. 2017. *PISA 2015 Results (Volume III): Students' well-being*. Paris: OECD Publishing. https://doi.org/10.1787/9789264273856-en. Accessed 16 February 2024.

Papi, Mostafa. 2010. The L2 motivational self system, L2 anxiety, and motivated behavior: A structural equation modelling approach. *System* 38 (3): 467–479. https://doi.org/10.1016/j.system.2010.06.011.

Papi, Mostafa, and Esmaeel Abdollahzadeh. 2012. Teacher motivational practice, student motivation, and possible L2 selves: An examination in the Iranian EFL context. *Language Learning* 62 (2): 571–594.

Payant, Caroline, Kim McDonough, Pakize Uludag, and Rachael Lindberg. 2019. Predicting integrated writing performance: Source comprehension, prewriting planning, and individual differences. *Journal of English for Academic Purposes* 40: 87–97. https://doi.org/10.1016/j.jeap.2019.06.001.

Pearson, William S. 2020. Mapping English language proficiency cut-off scores and pre-sessional EAP programmes in UK higher education. *Journal of English for Academic Purposes* 45: 100866. https://doi.org/10.1016/j.jeap.2020.100866.

Pekrun, Reinhard. 2006. The control-value theory of achievement emotions: Assumptions, corollaries, and implications for educational research and practice. *Educational Psychology Review* 18: 315–341. https://doi.org/10.1007/s10648-006-9029-9.

Poehner, M. E., M. Swain, and J. P. Lantolf, eds. 2018. *The Routledge handbook of sociocultural theory and second language development*. Boca Raton, FL: Routledge.

PourAli, PiriNaz, Maryam SeifNaraghi, and Ezatollah Naderi. 2017. Humanistic education and students' educational motivation in Tehran primary schools. *International Journal of Mental Health and Addiction* 15: 312–322. https://doi.org/10.1007/s11469-016-9703-1.

Prabhavathy, P., and S.N. Mahalakshmi. 2012. ELT with specific regard to humanistic approach. *Journal of Humanities and Social Sciences* 1 (1): 38–39. https://www.iosrjournals.org/iosr-jhss/papers/vol1-issue1/G0113839.pdf.

Pursewell, Katherine E. 2019. Humanistic learning theory in counselor education. *The Professional Counselor* 9 (4): 358–368. https://files.eric.ed.gov/fulltext/EJ1237586.pdf.

Rahman, Mehjabeen. 2013. Humanistic approaches' to language teaching: From theory to practice. *Stamford Journal of English* 4: 77–110. https://www.academia.edu/8219147/Humanistic_Approaches_to_Language_Teaching_from_Theory_to_Practice#:~:text=The%20paper%20explores%20humanistic%20approaches%20to%20language%20teaching%2C,theories%2C%20and%20their%20application%20in%20contemporary%20teaching%20practices.

Rajendram, Shakina, and Wenyangzi Shi. 2022. Supporting international graduate students' academic language and literacies development through online and hybrid communities of practice. *Journal of English for Academic Purposes* 60: 101178. https://doi.org/10.1016/j.jeap.2022.101178.

Reeve, John Marshall. 2009. Why teachers adopt a controlling motivating style toward students and how they can become more autonomy supportive. *Educational Psychologist* 44 (3): 159–175. https://doi.org/10.1080/00461520903028990.

Rogers, Carl R. 2001. The interpersonal relationship in the facilitation of learning. In *Supporting lifelong learning*, ed. Julia Clarke, Ann Hanson, Roger Harrison, and Fiona Reeve, 36–50. London: Routledge. https://www.perlego.com/book/1602283.

Rojas, Mariano, Alfonso Méndez, and Karen Watkins-Fassler. 2023. The hierarchy of needs empirical examination of Maslow's theory and lessons for development. *World Development* 165: 106185. https://doi.org/10.1016/j.worlddev.2023.106185.

Russo, Tom. 1995. Humanistic education and social action: Integrating knowing and caring. *Journal of Humanistic Education and Development* 34: 75–82. https://doi.org/10.1002/j.2164-4683.1995.tb00117.x.

Seligman, Martin E.P., Randal M. Ernst, Jane Gillham, Karen Reivich, and M. Mark Linkins. 2009. Positive education: Positive psychology and classroom interventions. *Oxford Review of Education* 35 (3): 293–311. https://doi.org/10.1080/03054980902934563.

Sharp, Aastair. 2012. Humanistic approaches to learning. In *Encyclopedia of the sciences of learning*, ed. Norbert M. Seel, 1469–1471. Boston, MA: Springer. https://doi.org/10.1007/978-1-4419-1428-6_530.

Slemp, Gavin R., Tan-Chyuan Chin, Margaret L. Kern, Christine Siokou, Daniel Loton, Lindsay G. Oades, Dianne Vella-Brodrick, and Lea Waters. 2017. Positive education in Australia: Practice, measurement, and future directions. In *Social and emotional learning in Australia and the Asia-Pacific: Perspectives, programs and approaches*, ed. Erica Frydenberg, Andrew J. Martin, and Rebecca J. Collie, 101–122. Singapore: Springer. https://doi.org/10.1007/978-981-10-3394-0_6.

Stevick, Earl. 2000. Autobiographical statement requested by CETESOL website for its "spotlight" section. Wayback Machine. https://web.archive.org/web/20161219021217/http:/celea.net/Resources/Documents/AFTERWORDS-9-AUTOBIO.pdf. Accessed 4 March 2025.

Stevick, Earl W. 1980. *Teaching languages, a way and ways*. Rowley, MA: Newbury House Publishers.

Stevick, Earl W. 1990. *Humanism in language teaching: a critical perspective*. Oxford University Press, Oxford

Stommel, Jesse. 2024. Ungrading. *Pedagogy: Critical Approaches to Teaching Literature, Language, Culture, and Composition* 24 (3): 327–340. https://muse.jhu.edu/article/944041.

Swain, Merrill, Penny Kinnear, and L. Linda Steinman. 2015. *Sociocultural theory in second language education: An introduction through narratives*, 2nd ed. Bristol: Multilingual Matters.

Thornton, Leslie J., and Mary Elizabeth McEntee. 2011. Staff development as self-development: Extension and application of Russo's humanistic-critical theory approach for humanistic education and social action integration. *The Journal of Humanistic Education and Development* 36 (3): 143–159. https://doi.org/10.1002/j.2164-4683.1998.tb00385.x.

Tilga, Henri, Vello Hein, Andre Koka, Kyra Hamilton, and Martin S. Hagger. 2019. The role of teachers' controlling behaviour in physical education on adolescents' health-related quality of life: Test of a conditional process model*. *Educational Psychology* 39 (7): 862–880. https://doi.org/10.1080/01443410.2018.1546830.

Tomlinson, Brian. 2008. Humanising an EAP textbook. *Humanising Language Teaching* 10 (2). http://old.hltmag.co.uk/apr08/sart01.htm.

van Compernolle, Remi A., and Laurence Williams. 2013. Sociocultural theory and second language pedagogy. *Language Teaching Research* 17 (3): 277–281. https://doi.org/10.1177/1362168813482933.

Van den Branden, Kris. 2012. Sustainable education: Basic principles and strategic recommendations. *School effectiveness and School Improvement* 23 (3): 285–304. https://doi.org/10.1080/09243453.2012.678865.

Viriya, Chorthip. 2018. Using task-based learning with students of academic English. *Arab World English Journal* 9 (4): 337–346. https://files.eric.ed.gov/fulltext/EJ1311226.pdf.

Wallace, Susan. 2015. *A dictionary of education*, 2nd ed. Oxford: Oxford University Press.

Western Governors University. 2020. What is humanistic learning theory in education. https://www.wgu.edu/blog/what-humanistic-learning-theory-education2007.html. Accessed 2 July 2025.

White, Mathew A., and Margaret L. Kern. 2018. Positive education: Learning and teaching for wellbeing and academic mastery. *International Journal of Wellbeing* 8 (1): 1–17. https://doi.org/10.5502/ijw.v8i1.588.

Wilson, Frances, Simon Child, and Irenka Suto. 2017. Assessing the transition between school and university: Differences in assessment between A level and university in English. *Arts and Humanities in Higher Education* 16 (2): 188–208. https://doi.org/10.1177/1474022216628302.

Wright, Gloria Brown. 2011. Student-centered learning in higher education. *International Journal of Teaching and Learning in Higher Education* 23 (2): 92–97. https://files.eric.ed.gov/fulltext/EJ938583.pdf.

Xu, Qi. 2021. Incorporating reading circles into a task-based EAP reading scheme. *ELT Journal* 75 (3): 341–350. https://doi.org/10.1093/elt/ccab012.

Yanita, Desi, and Sri Sumarni. 2024. Humanism: Goals, and beliefs addressed in English language teaching programs; literature review. *Jurnal Onoma: Pendidikan, Bahasa, dan Sastra* 10 (3): 3312–3331. https://e-journal.my.id/onoma/article/view/4108/2736.

3

EAP Contexts

3.1 EAP Contexts: A Brief Overview

Having introduced EAP and the role of humanism in education, this chapter explores the range of contexts in which EAP may be studied. It is important to consider the contexts in which EAP takes place as this can influence how EAP is applied and thus the potential for humanistic approaches to be applied. It could also allow for the practitioner to consider whether or how to apply these approaches. As the provision of EAP grows there has been a shift from the physical classroom support classes in an L1 English-speaking country to the variety of contexts and formats now seen globally. Whilst there are some unifying features of EAP globally, such as academic writing skills and the use of the English language itself, other aspects may vary significantly across contexts. An example of a feature which may vary is the teaching of reading skills in a face-to-face context as opposed to online. A face-to-face educator has the opportunity to model stages and monitor students whereas an online context perhaps may only be able to provide instructions or suggestions on reading skills. As a result of these different contexts, EAP may be applied differently and produce different learning outcomes. For these reasons this chapter looks at the range of contexts in which EAP takes

L. Dyer, *A Humanistic Approach to English for Academic Purposes Pedagogy*, https://doi.org/10.1007/978-3-032-00186-3_3

place and considers how this may influence pedagogy. Alexander et al. (2019) previously published a range of EAP contexts in their publication *EAP Essentials.* The authors listed three main categories with subdivisions:

- Context—syllabus goal, time and student aims
- People—learner motivation, teachers and the roles of students and teachers
- Content—language, language skills balance, materials, choice and use of texts and study skills

(Alexander et al. 2019)

Although many of the above remain pertinent to contemporary teaching and learning, others have developed in the years since publication. For example, Alexander et al. (2019) state that 'time' is inflexible but as is shown in Sects. 3.4.1 and 3.4.2 there is increasing flexibility in how EAP is studied. It is also noticeable that 'study skills' is the final subdivision and is listed as an 'other' skill. Based upon the information provided in Sect. 1.3, it could be argued that study or academic skills are now a significant feature of EAP provision and indeed an essential requirement. However, Alexander et al.'s (2019) list is still significant to today's EAP and this publication uses many of its subdivisions with additions to accommodate EAP's and education's changing face. For the purposes of this publication the following contexts will be reviewed in this chapter:

- Geographical location of the learning institution
- Institution type
- Level
- Specificity
- Timeliness
- Mode
- Value
- Duration
- Cohort language
- Cohort nationality

- The role of the teacher

These contexts are grouped as follows:

Physical contexts—This covers the contexts geographical location of the learning institution and institution type and relates to the physical nature of an educational provider. These physical factors are likely to be fixed, though there is potential for alterations such as through the opening of satellite campuses. The physical aspect is likely to play a role in EAP pedagogy which is discussed in Sect. 3.2.1.
Content contexts—Level and specificity relate to the content of an EAP course. The content may be determined by various parties, from the individual practitioner themselves through to higher level management and the students themselves. The content of an EAP course can play a role in how pedagogy is applied, with those courses requiring the completion of specific tasks being more restricted than one in which there is free reign over content.
Construct contexts—Timeliness, mode, value and duration can be considered part of the construction of an EAP programme. These may be determined by the EAP provider or perhaps even individual practitioners. On the other hand, these factors may be determined by higher levels such as by the institution or government. Each of the construct factors can determine pedagogy.
Demographic contexts—Both cohort language and cohort nationality fall into this category. Whilst it could be argued that these two contexts should be considered in Chapter 4 as they form part of an EAP student profile, they have been included in this chapter as they can play a role in determining EAP pedagogy. The role of the teacher is also covered in this category.

These contexts are not a complete all-encompassing representation of contemporary EAP contexts. However they reflect many of the settings and formats which both the student and practitioner find themselves in. Additionally, although the contexts have been separated out for explanation this is not a rigid dichotomy and there are chances for overlapping, as is the case where an EAP classroom may consist of learners undertaking the module on a compulsory basis and those who have chosen it as an option.

3.2 Physical Contexts

Physical contexts refer to where the learning takes place. These places are both the geographical location of the learning institution and the institution type itself. The drive for an international English education (Reynolds and Wei 2023) has led to EAP's expansion around the world through a plethora of educational providers. Both the geographical location and type of institution have the potential to influence how EAP pedagogy is approached.

3.2.1 Geographical Location of the Learning Institution

As a global language, perhaps one of the most apparent questions for EAP study is exactly where the provider is based. 'Base' refers to where the provider's main campus or corporate headquarters is located. This means that even if a student is studying in their home nation, the institution base of the provider may be different which in turn can influence their EAP experience. Whilst the selection of a learner's EAP provider is discussed in more detail in Sect. 4.4, this section looks at the location of the EAP provider and the impact that this may have on teaching and learning. The location of the EAP learning institution might influence the learning experience such as:

- The choice of topics through which EAP may be studied. For example, choosing topics relevant to Australian academia for students studying with Australian universities
- The local academic conventions which learners work towards
- Potential for exposure to the English language outside the classroom, such as studying at an English-speaking institution

As shown in Sect. 1.2, EAP has moved on from its roots in L1 English-speaking countries to a worldwide expansion, to which Kachru's three circles model (1985 cited by Kachru 1994) can be applied. The three circles model refers to three spheres of English based upon their geographical location. These spheres are

The inner circle—regions where the primary language is English, where the majority of speakers could be considered L1 speakers. These countries include Canada, the UK and Australia.
The outer circle—regions where English serves as a second language, a lingua franca or has significant historical importance. Countries in this category include India, Singapore and Nigeria
The expanding circle—regions where English is learned as a foreign language which covers the majority of locations worldwide.

These spheres in turn can be applied to the EAP provider, where the inner circle is a 'traditional' host country institution, the outer circle is an English significant context institution and the expanding circle can be referred to as EMI or TNE destinations.

3.2.1.1 The Traditional Host Countries—The Inner Circle

Kachru's inner circle can be applied to EAP institutions located in countries where English is the official majority or sole language. A group of six English-speaking countries, which are from the inner circle, are seen as the 'traditional' base for EAP: Australia, Canada, Ireland, New Zealand, the UK and the USA (Johnson and Tweedie 2021). In most instances this would require students to travel to one of the aforementioned destination countries to undertake their studies. These six destinations remain a popular choice for learners despite the global expansion of EAP. The offering of academic study in English can attract international students, with some such as Canada looking to increase their international student population (Johnson and Tweedie 2021). This in turn means a likelihood of increasing EAP provision. Students may also study at these institutions in other nations (see Sect. 3.2.2.2), which could be termed 'quasi-inner'. However, in these instances it is the institutional base which is likely to have the most significant oversight on teaching and learning. In terms of pedagogy, the type of EAP learners may receive is likely to be one that configures to the expected academic studies experience. That is to say the teaching of aspects such as critical thinking and writing in geo-academically acceptable rhetorics that caters for the specific needs of the individual host country.

It is noticeable that one group of English-speaking nations is missing from the traditional host countries—that of the English-speaking nations of the Caribbean. Despite being part of the inner circle, institutions in the Caribbean are often overlooked when discussing EAP provision. This is in spite of offering EAP based on British and American discourses (Milson-Whyte et al. 2021) to cater for both domestic and international students (Sanderson Cole 2012).

3.2.1.2 English Significant Contexts—The Outer Circle

The second set of destination countries are those where the English language plays a dominant role in society, even if it is not the most commonly spoken language in the country. Multilingual nations such as South Africa and Singapore operate much of their HE through the English language despite English not being the first language of the majority of their populations. In South Africa although there has been a move to promote the use of African languages in HE teaching and learning, the English language and EAP continues to provide learners with access to HE (Parkinson 2016). In Singapore, EAP has been implemented in the country's autonomous universities for both international and domestic students and this provision is inclusive of domestic students whose first language is English (Bo et al. 2022). EAP in the outer circle may conform to EAP inner circle norms or tailor towards what is conventional for their own locality.

3.2.1.3 EMI—The Expanding Circle

The final group locations are those which do not have English as one of their designated national or minority languages yet have institutions who offer some or all of their education through EMI. An institution may choose to offer their entire educational provision through EMI. Or EMI may only be offered for specific disciplines, standalone modules or offered partially as part of a bilingual programme (Swain and Johnson 1997). Through EMI, institutions are able to expand their student recruitment markets and become a place where learners come to study in English. Institutions may choose to implement EMI in their courses for a variety of reasons such as a wish to increase internationalisation and international visibility which in turn provide leverage in university rankings. International students may also pay higher tuition fees, such as in Sweden (Siegel 2022), which can increase institutional revenue and provide alternative sources of institutional income. In contrast, there may be no tuition fees, such as for those choosing to study in Norway (Wiers-Jenssen 2018), which may be attractive to students wishing to undertake their studies abroad. This subsequently may lead to an increase in EAP as institutions cater for learners to carry out academic studies through EMI. EAP in EMI contexts may follow either the EAP conventions in pace in inner circle locations or choose to adhere to practices that local institutions may abide by.

3.2.1.4 Questioning the Three Circles Model in EAP

Although there are many aspects of the three circles that could be considered relevant to EAP, there are questions over potential subordination. The notion of an inner circle suggests that this is the appropriate model for EAP with the outer and expanding circle aspiring to achieve that 'type' of EAP. As such it does not give credit the EAP produced by the outer and expanding circle (Xiaoqiong and Xianxing 2011). However, with EAP's increasing expansion in the outer and expanding circle there is momentum for a divergence from the inner circle norm and allow for multiple varieties of EAP to develop to cater for the needs of their specific context. Inner circle EAP may not consider non-Western epistemologies and therefore EAP outside this context can adapt for the academic community which it is catering for (Canagarajah 2014). Through applying a means analysis approach where courses are adapted to suit local situations (Holliday and Cooke 1982 cited by Jordan 1997), this suggests a potential splitting of EAP, much like that of EGAP and ESAP (see Sect. 3.3.2), specifically for local academic communities, e.g. English for Turkish Academic Purposes or English for Iranian Academic Purposes. The emergence of decolonisation in EAP supports the increasing recognition for both the outer and inner circle as well as multilingualism in the EAP classroom.

3.2.2 Institution Type

The next context for EAP is the institution type. For the purposes of this publication this is either purely public or purely private, both of which contain subdivisions. Institutions may have initially been set up by benefactors or collaboration between education driven individuals, such as those in the colonial USA (Lee 2017) or medieval England (University of Cambridge 2024). These institutions may have been considered as charitable organisations or even what is contemporarily thought of as private. However, even if institutions are labelled as public, there is an increasing reliance on private funding in the HE sector at a global level (Lee 2017). This context also considers the EAP that may happen in a disciplinary specific institution, such as those that may focus solely on Arts or STEM.

3.2.2.1 Public

There is no clear definition of what determines as educational institution to be classed as 'public' or state. However, in general, an institution can be defined as public if it is 'owned' by a government, serves public interests and is not for profit (Lee 2017). Although there is a global move towards privatisation of HE, universities in particular may still consider themselves to be public (Thornton 2011; Holmwood 2011). Public universities may be seen as the flagship for education and in many countries continue to attract significant student numbers, thus having the potential to attract more EAP students. The EAP courses in a public institution may be regulated by higher level governance or there may be scope for the provider to have some influence on course content and thus pedagogy.

3.2.2.2 Expansions Through the Quasi-Inner Circle—TNE and EMI

With the increasing internationalisation of tertiary education has arisen an increasing number of inner circle educational institutions opening 'bases' or satellite campuses outside their country of domain. This can be referred to as TNE or EMI if the language of instruction is English. A base can be a 'twinning' with a partner institution for a specific discipline or the creation of a new university campus (WTO 2010 cited in Li and Roberts 2012). These expansions have enabled learners to have an international education outside the domain country (British Council 2023). The education learners experience can take place in a range of different settings, as outlined in Table 3.1. One location where this type of educational internationalistation has become prevalent is China. To illustrate this, Li and Roberts (2012) outline the collaboration types of HE internationalisation which have taken place through the entry of UK universities in China and the impact that this can have on teaching and learning.

As the overseas teaching input increases, there is an expansion of teaching in the English language. As a result of this, the university ranking of the satellite campus can increase (Galloway and Ruegg 2020). This can result in an increase in the number of applicants who may require English language support through EAP provision. Despite the base of the satellite institution being located outside its operating location, it is the institutional base country that will most likely have the more significant impact on determining the learning experience (University of Nottingham Ningbo China 2024). Nevertheless, there is also potential for regulation by the host location.

Table 3.1 Collaboration types of UK universities in China

Collaboration type	Potential teaching and learning input	Role of English in teaching
Export	Raising awareness of a UK university with the aim of increasing student recruitment from China	Not applicable
Validation	A degree programme is run as a 2 + 2, where the first two years are completed in the partnered Chinese university. If a student performs well in the first two years, they may be issued an offer to complete their degree in the UK	English is the language of instruction for the UK component
Franchise	Also a split programme as in validation but where all students complete their degree in the UK. Visiting lecturers may attend from the UK university	Visiting lectures conducted in English and students complete their degree in the UK through English
Joint program	A further split programme but where the UK university delivers 50% of course delivery through allocating UK teaching staff to China for a designated teaching block	Lessons conducted by the UK university are delivered in English
Joint venture	The UK university opens a satellite campus (also known as an international branch campus (Lawton and Katsomitros 2012) in China with a curriculum that mirrors that of the UK base. Teaching is delivered by staff recruited specifically for the satellite campus	100% of teaching is in English

Adapted from Li and Roberts (2012)

3.2.2.3 Private

As with defining a public institution, there is no clearcut definition for a private one. In the modern era, an institution can be considered as private if it is not owned by a government, yet it may still be required to adhere to governmental regulations. It may also be a not for profit or alternatively a for profit institution (Lee 2017). In contrast to public institutions, private institutions may have more freedom to set their own institutional regulations, such as language of instruction, or even allow staff full reign over teaching content (Costa and Coleman 2012). In non-L1 English locations, many private institutions have opted to provide education through EMI, thus demanding a high proficiency in the language. This trend is noticeable in locations such as in Bangladesh (Islam and Stapa 2021), Saudi Arabia (Jamjoom 2016), Italy (Costa and Coleman 2012) and Oman (Issan 2016). These private institutions might provide English language training (i.e. EAP) or students may be required to have already attained the desired language ability in order to commence their studies. Students at private institutions may have an overall more positive approach to their learning, especially through EMI as they perceive overall greater benefits of learning through English and the reduction or removal of policies that may be in place in public institutions (Macaro and Akincioglu 2018). However, there are questions over EMI graduates and employability as they may need to revert to L1 to enter the job market. As stated previously, pedagogical practices should take into account the context in which they are operating to avoid clashes with local social, cultural and academic conventions (see Sect. 3.2.1.4).

3.2.2.4 Specialist Institutions

A specialist institution is one that offers courses in a particular specialism. Institutions in this category may specialise in areas such as performance and visual arts, STEM, veterinary science, medicine, business, humanities or military. A specialist institution may have stronger links to industry as they prepare their students for specific professions (Universities UK, n.d.). As a result, some of these institutions may have a small student population (Universities UK, n.d.); conversely, they may be on a larger scale to support the demand for training in such specialisms. Nevertheless, it is the specialism that can determine the approach taken to EAP provision. As specialist institutions, it is likely that many will take an ESAP approach (see Sect. 3.3.2.2), tailoring EAP to suit the specific needs of the institution specialism. However, this ESAP approach may be taken one step further within the specialism. ESAP allows for learners to explore the specificity of their discipline through EAP through contextualisation (see Sect. 3.3.2.2). However, institutional links to industry may divert learners away from what is seen as academic in their discipline to what is seen as purposeful for industry and future careers. It is therefore proposed that these institutions may currently be or have the potential to offer EAP that caters for the specific vocational training needs of the learner. This type of EAP could be labelled as ESVAP—English for Specific Vocational Academic Purposes—with the V to be replaced with the name of the student's academic discipline.

3.3 Content Contexts

These contexts consider the content of an EAP programme and its tailoring. These content contexts could be determined by the individual practitioner, the EAP provider, a higher level of governance or possibly the student. Both level and specificity fall into this category and can influence the pedagogy of an EAP course. For example an EGAP course for pre-undergraduates likely to have content that differs from that of an ESAP for pre-Master's level students. In both of these instances the EAP delivered is one that caters for the specific needs (disciplinary and level-wise) whilst providing content that is applicable to all (Hyland 2016).

3.3.1 Level

Level refers to the attainments and outputs that a learner is expected be able to achieve at a specific point in their educational journey (Wallace

2015). Whilst the majority of EAP takes place in HE, a minority does also take place at K-12 level (Lehman 2022; Riazi et al. 2020; Humphrey 2016). In HE terms, level determines what a learner should be able to do as they progress through their learning. That is to say a learner studying at taught postgraduate level should have obtained a higher skillset than a learner commencing their undergraduate studies. In line with academic educational qualification levels, EAP is also split into levels. The most common level of EAP is for undergraduate level (Riazi et al. 2020), with a PSP likely to prepare for entry to 1st year undergraduate level. Undergraduate ISP may provide support within levels undergraduate studies. For postgraduate studies EAP is often split to separately prepare students for entry to Master's degrees and for entry to doctorates. Without doubt there are overarching themes across these five levels such as the need to demonstrate critical thinking and referencing, but EAP for Master's level study may require students to demonstrate higher levels of criticality. Conversely EAP for doctoral study may have a much greater focus on speaking and writing than other skills considered less relevant to that level of study. Additionally, despite the variance between the aforementioned levels, it is also possible that undergraduates and postgraduates may also be placed in the same learning cohorts or all postgraduates may be placed together at the discretion of the EAP provider. This could be due to student numbers, teaching availability or course provision.

3.3.2 Specificity

This section considers how specificity plays a role in EAP provision. As a preparator or supporter of academic studies, EAP is designed to equip students with the requirements needed to successfully undertake academic studies. Whilst some skills, such as referencing, are considered essential for EAP learners progressing to any academic discipline, others could be considered to be discipline specific such as the writing of lab reports for STEM subjects. In order to cater for the encompassing and the discrete, EAP can be split into two strands according to its specificity—EGAP which caters for the encompassing and ESAP catering for the discrete (Hyland 2016).

3.3.2.1 EGAP

EGAP's original construction was one of language and skills that were considered as transferrable to academic study such as reading strategies and note-making (Monbec 2020). EGAP is the norm for many institutions and is also often used as a means for accommodating cohorts from a variety of academic disciplines (Gardiner 2016 cited in Monbec 2020). Moreover, it may be offered simultaneously to ESAP courses where ESAP courses have been produced for some disciplines but with other students undertaking EGAP. This could be due to institutional provision, absence of expertise or low demand for ESAP in some disciplines. An EGAP context aims to give the learner an all-round learning experience which may focus on linguistic acquirements and structural features of academic discourse presentation (Yasuda 2023). It can prove beneficial for learners who are not yet ready to enter their disciplinary discourse community (Heron and Webster 2019). EGAP is based upon assumed academic and linguistic necessities. However, it may not provide learners with specificities for their academic studies. One example could be the discouragement of the use of the pronoun 'I' in academic written discourse, yet many disciplines may allow its use.

3.3.2.2 ESAP

On the concentrated side of EAP there has emerged the ESAP approach. There has been a trend in institutions providing more discipline specific EAP or ESAP (Hyland 2016). Examples of ESAP include language for the sciences, language for the arts and language for law. These courses allow learners to explore specific features of their discipline and learn how to apply them in their academic studies. Writing in particular is an area in which the rhetoric can vary greatly across the disciplines and the specificity required to cover what is needed in academic field is unlikely to be entirely covered in an EGAP course. As mentioned Sect. 3.3.2.1, although an EGAP course may instruct learners to avoid the pronoun 'I' in their writing, many arts disciplines or reflective tasks may encourage the use of it. An ESAP course can tailor content to suit the needs of the discipline and can include the use of the pronoun 'I' if required. Through ESAP institutions can provide learners with more focused and pertinent content than that of an EGAP course. For example, ESAP writing may look at traits for the specific discipline, such as concision in STEM or the use of metaphors in language studies. It has been acknowledged that the contextualising of EAP within disciplines has been beneficial and improves scaffolding through to academic studies (Godfrey and Whong 2020). It may also prove to be engaging and motivating for learners to take that first step into discovering and applying the linguistic requirements and skills necessary for their future studies, thus visualising their future ideal self (see Sect. 2.5.2.4). However, ESAP raises questions over the use of non-specialists (i.e. the EAP practitioner) educating learners in a field in which they themselves are not experts. If a student requires help with a written task on an advanced topic, the EAP teacher would be able to help with its EAP-ness but may struggle to understand the content which is integrated into the discourse. This could cause issues when the EAP teacher supports the EAP-ness of the work but the result may interfere with the disciplinary content the student is conveying. A further complication of ESAP is that it may only be seen as support for disciplines (Hyland 2016) rather than the higher skill training that it actually is. This could be especially applicable in ISP situations where content input is valued over language output. ESAP may also prove to be too challenging to learners who may be intending to undertake a field of academic study ab initio and would instead benefit from a more general approach (Hyland 2016).

3.4 Construct Contexts

The term construct has multiple understandings in EAP. For example it has been used to describe dimensions around assessment (Macqueen 2022) and the shift from EGAP to ESAP (Baffy 2017). For this chapter, construct contexts are considered to be the management side of an EAP programme. That is to say addressing areas such as when a programme should run, how long for, how it is delivered to the learner and what is deemed to be the programme's worth.

3.4.1 Timeliness

In general terms EAP provision is divided into two formats: that which takes place as preparation for academic studies (i.e. PSP) and that which takes place concurrently with academic studies (i.e. ISP). EAP that is integrated into a course or is taken as an optional extra during studies relates to ISP as they occur concurrently to academic studies. This is even the case for EAP an IFP, which although is a preparatory course for undergraduate studies, can be classified as a form of ISP as it supports learning in other modules and the course itself is a standalone construction (Stazicker and Woods 2022). Both PSP and ISP courses may be general or discipline specific EAP (see Sect. 3.3.2).

3.4.1.1 PSP

PSPs are the most common form of EAP course. PSP is end-goal oriented (Tibbetts and Chapman 2023), devised to meet the needs of the target (Munby 1978 cited by Jordan 1997) of undertaking academic studies through the English language and designed to be the sole study focus for learners. They can take the form of intensive courses of up to a full academic year and they are mostly likely to immediately be followed by entry to the student's academic program, although it is also possible that there may be a gap between the PSP and beginning academic studies. However, perhaps the most important aspect of a PSP is when it takes place. In other words a PSP takes places prior to a course of academic studies and is considered to be a preparator this. It is therefore the function of a PSP to elevate a learner to a threshold of EAP that is considered suitable for entry to academic studies that will be carried out through the medium of English. Thus a PSP teaches the language and skills that are considered necessary for academic study. These skills may be revisited several times during the course of the PSP, either as designated course content or at the behest of teachers and learners. PSPs are likely to have some form of assessment to determine student progression to academic studies (Seviour 2015). Assessment on a PSP may take the form of high weighted culminative summative tasks such as writing and speaking assessments being at 50% of the final grade respectively, or assessment may be drawn out over a wider range of tasks with lower weightings such as through a portfolios.

3.4.1.2 ISP

ISPs contrast in timeliness to PSPs. An ISP is designed to cater for students who require or desire extra support during their academic studies and take place concurrently with these. The course is most likely to focus on academic writing as this is the most common form of assessment for most academic disciplines (Tibbetts and Chapman 2023). In a discipline specific ISP, content may be drawn directly from degree syllabi or from departmental teaching staff who direct EAP practitioners as to what they would like ISP students to produce (Tibbetts and Chapman 2023). Discipline specific ISPs may be funded directly by academic departments or by the institution itself. An ISP may consist of a succession of standalone sessions, hence the learner would not miss out on sequential information should they miss a lesson. On the other hand, sessions may be sequential and take learners through scaffolding phases designed to directly support academic studies. An ISP is unlikely to have its own specific assessment but may be integrated into disciplinary assessment through the inclusion of 'language' as one of the marking criterium (Tibbetts and Chapman 2023).

3.4.2 Mode

The context of mode considers the environment in which the learners are taught or study. Mode can refer to face-to-face learning, online learning, hybrid learning and distance learning or an interchangeable combination of any to allow for both synchronous and asynchronous learning experiences (Beckingham 2024). Mode can also refer to whether a programme is studied as full or part time.

3.4.2.1 Face-to-Face

Due its emergence as support for the international student in the pre-digital inner circle university (see Sect. 1.2), it was the norm for EAP to take place in a face-to-face learning environment. Additionally, despite advances in digital education face-to-face teaching and learning was the dominant mode for HE until the COVID-19 pandemic (Daumiller et al. 2021). EAP face-to-face provides the learner and educator with an environment that allows for real time monitoring and scaffolding of tasks. Unless we as practitioners have been specifically trained to teach in an online environment, it is face-to-face teaching that we have been primed for. As such, the pedagogy produced for EAP is one that is enabled for being in a face-to-face context.

3.4.2.2 Online

Whereas a face-to-face intensive context may provide students with a 'prescriptive language curriculum' (Rajendram and Shi 2022, p. 17), an online learning experience by nature encourages learner autonomy and a pedagogical approach suited to that context. In online learning, the face-to-face element, also known as synchronous teaching and learning, is likely to be less than that of a physical face-to-face. In contrast, learning which is carried out outside synchronous classes is known as asynchronous. A key aspect of online learning that has developed is flipped learning where learning resources and activities can be accessed and carried out asynchronously prior to the designated 'class' time (Pickering and Roberts 2017). Flipped learning has been viewed positively by learners as it developed learner autonomy and a heightened level of self-regulation (Villegas 2021). A further aspect of online contexts is that it provides opportunities for the development of CoPs. CoPs may be developed in order to support student learning and avoid a sense of isolation alongside developing the desired languages and literacies (Rajendram and Shi 2022). Furthermore, CoPs have been shown to develop learner autonomy, agency and confidence (Rajendram and Shi 2022). They can aid the learning process through peer interaction and support (Asoodar et al. 2014). They also allow for students to build relationships through linguistic means with others, especially those who may not speak their language (Rajendram and Shi 2022) as the asynchronisity gives the learner time to create their outputs such as online posts.

3.4.2.3 Hybrid and Blended Learning

The terms hybrid and blended learning can be problematic in their definitions. They may generally be considered as learning that allows learners to mix online learning with face-to-face sessions (Coursera 2023). This could be written into a course curriculum or may be undertaken as a necessity such as in the closing stages of the COVID-19 pandemic when students may have been able to attend some face-to-face sessions but were otherwise expected to study online. However, for hybrid learning some institutions have a different perspective and use this term to refer to courses where there are separate online and classroom based cohorts that are undertaking the same concurrent course of study (University of Edinburgh 2024). This may allow for some form of collaboration between the cohorts. Whatever the definition may be, it can be said that hybrid learning involves some form of learning at a distance from the educational provider and thus the curriculum reflects activities which the learner undertakes independently. Regarding blended, this may be used interchangeably with the term hybrid but perhaps clearer in explaining its construct as the learning experience for each student involved is both online and face-to-face (Wallace 2015). This method may have online and face-to-face teaching separated into blocks, such as the first half of a course being entirely online and the second entirely face-to-face. Alternatively the online and face-to-face elements may be mixed throughout the course. Whichever approach is taken, educational providers must be able to account for their reasons to provide blended or hybrid modes of teaching and learning (Palikat and Gruba 2021) and this the online component of a programme should be learner-centred (Eskildsen and Theodórsdóttir 2015).

3.4.2.4 Distance

Whilst in the past distance learning meant studying by correspondence, with the quality of teaching materials generally considered lower than that offered in face-to-face situations (Coursera 2023), it has now generally been replaced by online learning (Wallace 2015).

3.4.2.5 Full Time

In terms of PSPs, it can be said that for the most part these are offered on a solely full time basis, meaning that EAP is the sole focus in the learner's studies. More details on this can be found in Sect. 3.4.1.1.

3.4.2.6 Part Time

It is less common for a PSP to be offered on a part time basis. However it may become a de facto part time course depending on how it is delivered, such as in an online learning context where the student manages the majority of their own study time. Although a teacher may allocate a specific number of hours of independent study for specific tasks, it may take the learner less time than expected. Thus the student may actually end up studying part time hours. However, in the case of 'real' part time programmes, multiple aspects need to be considered that contrast with full time study. Some examples are:

- Scheduling—does a part time PSP consist of just morning or afternoon sessions? Or is teaching compressed into perhaps two full days a week?
- Course content—How long is the part time course? For example, if a part time PSP runs alongside a full time PSP, how is content selected for the part time student? In contrast, is a part time PSP more protracted in order to cover the content of its full time equivalent?
- Course cohort—do part time learners study alongside full time students or are they kept separate?

- Entry level—do students need to achieve a higher level to study part time? Are they considered to be more capable to carry out independent study and manage their own learning?
- Engagement—how can engagement in the EAP course be maintained alongside other drivers in a student's life?

In contrast to PSP, an ISP is part time as it runs alongside the student's academic studies. More details on ISPs can be found in Sect. 3.4.1.2.

3.4.3 Value

The value context addresses the merit placed on a unit of learning by a learning institution, with those contributing towards eventual qualification outcomes holding credits. Depending on context, EAP courses can be identified as having the following values: credit bearing, compulsory but not credit bearing, gatekeeping and optional (Charles and Pecorari 2015). Each of these values could potentially impact on curricula as well as learner engagement.

3.4.3.1 Credit Bearing

Credit bearing EAP courses have been introduced at many institutions, where a module in EAP forms part of the final qualification grading in academic studies. These credit bearing courses may be compulsory or optional, but as they are designated to hold credit content may be prescriptive in order to meet the specified requirements that students are expected to achieve. As such there is chance for a greater possibility of administrators being part of decision making over curriculum content (Heydon and Wang 2006). Whilst there is no strict requisite for what could be deemed as essential for a credit bearing EAP programme, it is generally expected that there will be some form of oral assessment, most likely a presentation (Palmour 2023), alongside significant focus on reading and writing development. However, this means that courses may not be developed with the specific needs of the student cohort in mind (Huang 2024).

3.4.3.2 Compulsory But Not Credit Bearing

In a compulsory but not credit bearing EAP course, learners may be required to reach a specific attendance level in order to pass or fail. A fail may result in the need to retake the course but does not affect the outcome of the student's progression through their academic studies (Ataç et al. 2018). On the other hand, the English language component may need to be passed in order to progress through or graduate from an educational institution (University of Hong Kong 2024). The integration of English language courses into a curriculum can vary by country, region, institution, academic department or discipline level. Whilst in many of these contexts learners may study 'general English', English for specific or academic purposes may be put forward where deemed appropriate or subject to availability. In Taiwan for example, the government implemented English Language Education Policy requires all HE students to achieve a minimum threshold before they are able to graduate from university (Rüdiger et al. 2022), with a growing emphasis on discipline specific EAP (Chang 2017). One discipline which has widely implemented English language training is medicine, such as in France where is has been compulsory since 1992 (Rannou et al. 2007) and in Japan where English for specific purposes has been promoted in the nation's medical and dental schools (Rodis et al. 2014).

3.4.3.3 Gatekeeping

Defined as controlling who gets access to resources or opportunities (Cambridge Dictionary 2024), gatekeeping in academic studies can inhibit students from progressing to the next stage of their learning. Whilst many institutions prefer to use an international English language exam such as the gatekeeper for course entry, there are some who use their EAP PSPs as a second gatekeeper. Failure of all or part of an EAP course may result in a student resitting or non-progression to academic studies (Pearson 2020). This means that not only do students need to satisfy international examination entry requirements, they also need to 'pass' the EAP course to progress to academic studies. Following along the same lines as compulsory EAP courses, gatekeeping courses may too have less freedom in their course design as they function as a means for students to meet those specific entry requirements determined by policy makers external to EAP. This can lead to potential washback through a restricted curriculum (Green 2007). Through washback, a curriculum is influenced by testing (Barnes 2017) and therefore may not need the actual needs of learners.

3.4.3.4 Optional EAP

The design of an optional EAP programme can be influenced by multiple factors such target audience, scheduling of classes and the desired learning outcomes. As writing is one of the most frequently covered skills in EAP (Hirvela 2016), it would not be uncommon for an optional EAP class to be solely focused on this.

3.4.4 Duration

The duration of an EAP course can depend on a variety of factors, namely whether it is a PSP or ISP. Thus this context links strongly with Timeliness. This section considers the duration of both PSP and ISP.

3.4.4.1 PSP

The duration of PSPs can vary significantly in length, from short intensive courses of a matter of weeks to year-long programmes of study. Short intensive courses may be used for institution applicants who fall just slightly short of English language entry requirements (see Sect. 4. 3). These intensive courses, of perhaps 4–6 weeks, have been shown to have a meaningful impact on student outcomes (Mazgutova and Hanks 2021; Wright et al. 2022). This is because the immersive contexts provide fostering condition to develop linguistic competence, critical thinking and content knowledge (Wright et al. 2022). For a short intensive course, content would be carefully selected designed to allow for learners to achieve the desired outcomes in the timeframe. In contrast, PSPs may also take a longer intensive format. Although careful content and planning would also be needed for longer PSPs, the timeframe may allow for repetition of tasks and deeper immersion into EAP, catering specifically to student needs.

3.4.4.2 ISP

As with PSPs, the duration of ISPs can differ in duration. In some contexts, ISPs may only be offered on a semesterly basis whereas others may provide support for the full duration of academic studies (see Sect. 3.4.1).

3.5 Demographic Contexts

As stated previously, it could be considered more suitable to review these contexts in Chapter 4 which focuses on building a profile of the EAP learner. However, the demographic of a cohort of EAP students can itself influence the pedagogy of a course as outlined below.

3.5.1 Cohort Language

Cohort language is an important aspect to consider in EAP contexts. A monolingual cohort may be formed of entirely L1 English speakers (or speakers that could be considered bilingual English speakers) or L1 speakers of another language. For the L1 English speakers, there may be less need for input linguistic factors such as grammar but rather the focus may be on register and genre (Stazicker and Woods 2022). This could also mean increased focus on content and skills such as referencing. For a monolingual group of non-L1 speakers English, there may be a necessity for more linguistic input, depending on the language level of the cohort. If the cohort's level of English is not at the required level, language input would form part of the syllabus.

A multilingual cohort may prove more challenging to teach than a monolingual one as it raises a wider variety of issues that may not be seen in the monolingual group. A multilingual cohort may consist of individuals with varying linguistic needs or gaps which may be linked to their L1. In designing EAP courses, an awareness of L1 and English divergences could be beneficial for the learner and educator alike.

3.5.2 Cohort Nationality

The global expansion of EAP has similarly affected the nationality mix of student cohorts. As stated in Sect. 3.2.1.1, in the past EAP students were most likely to have travelled to an inner circle destination to undertake their studies, increasing the likelihood of there being a mix of nationalities. However, as the number of EAP providers expands worldwide there is greater potential for cohorts to be made up of a single nationality. Course content for a multinational cohort may differ from a single nationality group (Stazicker and Woods 2022). For a multinational group, syllabus design would reflect and be accessible to different cultural backgrounds. In contrast, the shared experience of a single nationality cohort can tailor content to that specific group of students (Canagarajah 2014) which may not be understandable to outsiders.

3.5.3 The Role of the Teacher

The purpose of this publication is to provide practitioners with an alternative approach to EAP pedagogy and a framework (PPCP) through which they can apply it. However, it is recognised that a one size fits all approach does not work (Cavanagh et al. 2019), thus this publication is not a manual for the practitioner on how to teach pedagogy. Yet it is recognised that the teacher can have an impact on the learning experience. Pedagogical choices have the potential to influence student achievement (Burridge 2014). A self-review of teaching practice can allow for teachers to consider which areas of instruction may benefit from the use of alternative pedagogies, with alternative pedagogies having the potential to enhance student learning (Burridge 2014; Meguid and Collins 2017; Wake et al. 2023). Section 4.5.4.5 provides details on how a teacher may impact on a student's learning experience.

3.6 Concluding the Contexts

Contexts play a significant role in determining EAP pedagogy and must be considered before employing any humanistic practices. As stated at the beginning of this chapter, these chosen EAP contexts are not all encompassing and it is recognised that others may exist. It is also recognised that each of the contexts themselves are not comprehensive (for example, Sect. 3.2.2 does not consider dual public-private institutions). However, what this chapter does provide is an overview of what could be considered the common contexts in which EAP operates and that each of these individual contexts combine together to influence teaching and learning produce the EAP experience. It is in the next chapter that the potential impact these contexts have on the student are reviewed.

References

Alexander, Olwyn, Sue Argent, and Jenifer Spence. 2019. *EAP essentials: A teacher's guide to principles and practice*, 2nd ed. Reading: Garnet.

Asoodar, Maryam, Mahmood Reza Atai, Shahin Vaezi, and Suyyedeh Susan Marandi. 2014. Examing effectiveness in community of practice of online English for academic purposes (EAP) assessment in virtual classes. *Computers and Education* 70: 291–300. https://doi.org/10.1016/j.compedu.2013.08.016.

Ataç, Bengü Aksu, Hatice Özgan Sucu, Baris Eriçok, and Merve Bulut. 2018. The identification of difference between achievement levels of optional and compulsory English preparatory class students. *The Journal of Language and Linguistic Studies* 14 (3): 269–280. https://eric.ed.gov/?id=EJ1193271.

Baffy, Marta. 2017. Shifting frames to construct a Legal English class. *Journal of English for Academic Purposes* 25: 58–70. https://doi.org/10.1016/j.jeap.2016.11.003.

Barnes, Melissa. 2017. Washback: Exploring what constitutes "good" teaching practices. *Journal of English for Academic Purposes* 30: 1–12. https://doi.org/10.1016/j.jeap.2017.10.003.

Beckingham, Sue. 2024. Re-defining modes of learning. In *How to use digital learning with confidence and creativity: A practical introduction*, ed. Gearóid

Ó Súilleabháin, Donna Lanclos, and Tom Farrelly, 168–177. Cheltenham: Edward Elgar. https://doi.org/10.4337/9781035311293.00034.

Bo, Wenjin Vikki, Lyndon Lim, and Yuna Lin. 2022. An investigation of multilingual domestic university student perceptions of English for academic purposes. *Behavioral Sciences* 12 (9): 328. https://doi.org/10.3390/bs1209 0328.

British Council. 2023. Studying for a UK degree in the UAE. https://study-uk.britishcouncil.org/plan-studies/ways-learning/degree-outside-uk/uae. Accessed 19 December 2023.

Burridge, Peter. 2014. Understanding teachers' pedagogical choice: A sociological framework combining the work of Bourdieu and Giddens. *Educational Studies* 40 (5): 571–589. https://doi.org/10.1080/03055698.2014.953915.

Cambridge Dictionary. 2024. Gatekeeping. https://dictionary.cambridge.org/dictionary/english/gatekeeping. Accessed 7 March 2024.

Canagarajah, Suresh. 2014. EAP in Asia: Challenges and possibilities. In *English for academic purposes (EAP): Negotiating appropriate practices in a global context*, ed. Indika Liyanage and Tony Walker, 93–102. Rotterdam: Brill.

Cavanagh, Michael, Jennifer Barr, Robyn Moloney, Rod Lane, Iain Hay, and Hye-Eun Chu. 2019. Pre-service teachers' impact on student learning: Planning, teaching, and assessing during professional practice. *The Australian Journal of Teacher Education* 44 (2): 66–81. https://eric.ed.gov/?id=EJ1 207744.

Chang, Karen Chung-chien. 2017. From EAP to ESP: A teacher's identity development. *Taiwan Journal of TESOL* 14 (2): 1–100. https://files.eric.ed.gov/fulltext/EJ1171158.pdf.

Charles, Maggie, and Diane Pecorari. 2015. *Introducing English for academic purposes*. London: Routledge. https://doi.org/10.4324/9781315682129.

Costa, Francesca, and James A. Coleman. 2012. A survey of English-medium instruction in Italian higher education. *International Journal of Bilingual Education and Bilingualism* 16 (1): 3–19. https://doi.org/10.1080/136 70050.2012.676621.

Coursera. 2023. What is distance learning: And is it for you? https://www.cou rsera.org/articles/distance-learning. Accessed 12 January 2024.

Daumiller, Martin, Raven Rinas, Julia Hein, Stefan Janke, Oliver Dickhäuser, and Markus Dresel. 2021. Shifting from face-to-face to online teaching during COVID-19: The role of university faculty achievement goals for attitudes towards this sudden change, and their relevance for burnout/

engagement and student evaluations of teaching quality. *Computers in Human Behavior* 118: 106677. https://doi.org/10.1016/j.chb.2020.106677.

Eskildsen, Søren. W., and GuÐrún Theodórsdóttir. 2015. Constructing L2 learning spaces: Ways to achieve learning inside and outside the classroom. *Applied Linguistics* 38 (2): 143–165. https://doi.org/10.1093/applin/amv010.

Galloway, Nicola, and Rachael Ruegg. 2020. The provision of student support on English medium instruction programmes in Japan and China. *Journal of English for Academic Purposes* 45: 100846. https://doi.org/10.1016/j.jeap.2020.100846.

Godfrey, Jeanne, and Melinda Whong. 2020. A collaborative scholarship model of EAP research and practice. In *What is good academic writing? Insights into discipline-specific student writing*, ed. Melinda Whong and Jeanne Godfrey, 9–30. London: Bloomsbury. https://www.bloomsbury.com/uk/what-is-good-academic-writing-9781350110380/.

Green, Anthony. 2007. Washback to learning outcomes: A comparative study of IELTS preparation and university pre-sessional language courses. *Assessment in Education: Principles, Policy and Practice* 14 (1): 75–97. https://doi.org/10.1080/09695940701272880.

Heron, Marion, and Joanne Webster. 2019. Scaffolding talk in EAP lessons: An examination of experienced teachers' practices. *Innovation in Language Learning and Teaching* 13 (4): 358–370. https://doi.org/10.1080/17501229.2018.1466892.

Heydon, Rachel M., and Ping Wang. 2006. Curricular ethics in early childhood education programming: A challenge to the Ontario Kindergarten Program. *McGill Journal of Education/Revue des sciences de l'éducation de McGill* 41 (1). https://mje.mcgill.ca/article/view/508.

Hirvela, Alan. 2016. Academic reading into writing. In *The Routledge handbook of English for academic purposes*, ed. Ken Hyland and Philip Shaw, 127–138. London: Routledge. https://doi.org/10.4324/9781315657455.

Holmwood, John. 2011. The idea of a public university. In *A manifesto for the public university*, ed. John Holmwood, 12–26. London: Bloomsbury.

Huang, Ju Chuan. 2024. Unveiling EFL graduate students' EAP needs and perceptions of EAP courses: A large-scale survey in Taiwan. *Journal of English for Academic Purposes* 68: 101348. https://doi.org/10.1016/j.jeap.2024.101348.

Humphrey, Sally. 2016. EAP in school settings. In *The Routledge handbook of English for academic purposes*, ed. Ken Hyland and Philip Shaw, 447–460. London: Routledge. https://doi.org/10.4324/9781315657455.

Hyland, Ken. 2016. General and specific EAP. In *The Routledge handbook of English for academic purposes*, ed. Ken Hyland and Philip Shaw, 17–29. London: Routledge. https://doi.org/10.4324/9781315657455.
Islam, Md Shaiful, and Mahani Bt Stapa. 2021. Students' low proficiency in spoken English in private universities in Bangladesh: Reasons and remedies. *Language testing in Asia* 11 (1). https://doi.org/10.1186/s40468-021-00139-0.
Issan, Salha A. 2016. The obstacles and challenges of private education in the Sultanate of Oman. In *A global perspective on private higher education*, ed. Mahsood Shah and Chenicheri Sid Nair, 205–217. London: Chandos Publishing. https://doi.org/10.1016/B978-0-08-100872-0.00012-4.
Jamjoom, Yussra. 2016. Private higher education and graduate employability. In *A global perspective on private higher education*, ed. Mahsood Shah and Chenicheri Sid Nair, 189–204. London: Chandos Publishing. https://doi.org/10.1016/B978-0-08-100872-0.00011-2.
Johnson, Robert C., and M. Gregory Tweedie. 2021. "IELTS-out/TOEFL-out": Is the end of general English for academic purposes near? Tertiary student achievement across standardized tests and general EAP. *Interchange* 52: 101–113. https://doi.org/10.1007/s10780-021-09416-6.
Jordan, R. R. 1997. *English for academic purposes. A guide and resource book for teachers*. Cambridge: Cambridge University Press.
Kachru, Braj B. 1994. Englishization and contact linguistics. *World Englishes* 13 (2): 135–154. https://doi.org/10.1111/j.1467-971X.1994.tb00303.x.
Lawton, William Andrew, and Alex Katsomitros. 2012. International branch campuses: Data and developments. The Observatory on Borderless Higher Education. https://www.researchgate.net/publication/225083589_International_Branch_Campuses_Data_and_Developments/link/5f228fbd299bf13404927ed7/download?_tp=eyJjb250ZXh0Ijp7ImZpcnN0UGFnZSI6InB1YmxpY2F0aW9uIiwicGFnZSI6InB1YmxpY2F0aW9uIn19. Accessed 8 April 2024.
Lee, Young-Joo. 2017. Understanding higher education institutions' publicness: Do public universities produce more public outcomes than private universities? *Higher Education Quarterly* 71 (2): 182–203. https://doi.org/10.1111/hequ.12120.
Lehman, Clayton. 2022. Examining teacher opinions of age and duration of English language support in international schools. *Journal of English Teaching* 8 (1): 169–181. https://doi.org/10.33541/jet.v8i1.3517.
Li, Xiaoqing, and Joanne Roberts. 2012. A stages approach to the internationalization of higher education? The entry of UK universities into China. *The*

Service Industries Journal 32 (7): 1011–1038. https://doi.org/10.1080/02642069.2012.662495.

Macaro, Ernesto, and Mustafa Akincioglu. 2018. Turkish university students' perceptions about English medium instruction: Exploring year group, gender and university type as variables. *Journal of Multilingual and Multicultural Development* 39 (3): 256–270. https://doi.org/10.1080/01434632.2017.1367398.

Macqueen, Susy. 2022. Construct in assessments of spoken language. In *Handbook of language assessment across modalities*, ed. Tobias Haug, Wolfgang Mann, and Ute Knoch, 233–248. Oxford: Oxford University Press. https://doi.org/10.1093/oso/9780190885052.003.0020.

Mazgutova, Diana, and Judith Hanks. 2021. L2 learners' perceptions of their writing strategies on an intensive EAP course. *Journal of Academic Writing* 11 (1): 45–61. https://doi.org/10.18552/joaw.v11i1.566.

Meguid, Eiman Abdel, and Matthew Collins. 2017. Students' perceptions of lecturing approaches: Traditional versus interactive teaching. *Advances in Medical Education and Practice* 8: 229–240. https://doi.org/10.2147/AMEP.S131851.

Milson-Whyte, Vivette, Raymond Oenbring, and Brianne Jaquette. 2021. Weh wi deh/veh vi is/where we are: Teaching and researching academic writing in the Caribbean. *Composition Studies* 49 (3): 160–164. https://files.eric.ed.gov/fulltext/EJ1337595.pdf.

Monbec, Laetitia. 2020. Systemic functional linguistics for the EGAP module: Revisiting the common core. *Journal of English for Academic Purposes* 43: 100794. https://doi.org/10.1016/j.jeap.2019.100794.

Palikat, Cynthia Nicholas, and Paul Gruba. 2021. *Sustainability of blended language learning programs*. London: Routledge. https://www.perlego.com/book/3055864.

Palmour, Louise. 2023. Assessing oral presentations: An analysis of score-reaching dialogue between EAP practitioners. *Journal of English for Academic Purposes* 62: 101210. https://doi.org/10.1016/j.jeap.2022.101210.

Parkinson, Jean. 2016. EAP in multilingual English-dominant contexts. In *The Routledge handbook of English for academic purposes*, ed. Ken Hyland and Philip Shaw, 84–96. London: Routledge. https://doi.org/10.4324/9781315657455.

Pearson, William S. 2020. Mapping English language proficiency cut-off scores and pre-sessional EAP programmes in UK higher education. *Journal of English for Academic Purposes* 45: 100866. https://doi.org/10.1016/j.jeap.2020.100866.

Pickering, James D., and David J.H. Roberts. 2017. Flipped classroom or an active lecture? *Clinical Anatomy* 31 (1): 118–121. https://doi.org/10.1002/ca.22983.

Rajendram, Shakina, and Wenyangzi Shi. 2022. Supporting international graduate students' academic language and literacies development through online and hybrid communities of practice. *Journal of English for Academic Purposes* 60: 101178. https://doi.org/10.1016/j.jeap.2022.101178.

Rannou, François, Jean-Pierre. Charpy, Didier Carnet, Serge Poiraudeau, and Marie-Annick. Hamonet. 2007. Medical English in medical school: The French experience. *La Presse médicale* 36 (5 Pt 1): 794–798. https://doi.org/10.1016/j.lpm.2006.09.022.

Reynolds, Barry Lee, and Rining Wei. 2023. Global English education and EAP research in the new era: An introduction. *International Journal of English for Academic Purposes: Research and Practice* 3 (2): 69–73. https://doi.org/10.3828/ijeap.2023.4.

Riazi, A. Mehdi., Hessameddin Ghanbar, and Ismaeil Fazel. 2020. The contexts, theoretical and methodological orientation of EAP research: Evidence from empirical articles published in the Journal of English for Academic Purposes. *Journal of English for Academic Purposes* 48: 100925. https://doi.org/10.1016/j.jeap.2020.100925.

Rodis, Omar M.M., Edward Barroga, J. Patrick Barron, James Hobbs, Jayanetti A. Jayawardena, Ikuo Kageyama, Bukasa Kalubi, Clive Langham, Yoshizo Matsuka, Yoichiro Miyake, Naoko Seki, Hiroko Oka, Martin Peters, Yo Shibata, Roxana Stegaroiu, Kazuyoshi Suzuki, Shigeru Takahashi, Hironori Tsuchiya, Toshiko Yoshida, and Katsuhiko Yoshimoto. 2014. A proposed core curriculum for dental English education in Japan. *BMC Medical Education* 14 (1): 239–239. https://doi.org/10.1186/s12909-014-0239-4.

Rüdiger, Sofia, Jakob R.E. Leimgruber, and Ming-I Lydia Tseng. 2022. English in Taiwan—Expanding the scope of corpus-based research on East Asian Englishes. *English Today* 39 (2): 100–109. https://doi.org/10.1017/S0266078422000062.

Sanderson Cole, Karen. 2012. Promoting cooperative learning in an expository writing course. *Journal of International Education Research* 8 (2): 113–124. https://doi.org/10.19030/jier.v8i2.6831.

Seviour, Martin. 2015. Assessing academic writing on a pre-sessional EAP course: Designing assessment which supports learning. *Journal of English for Academic Purposes* 18: 84–89. https://doi.org/10.1016/j.jeap.2015.03.007.

Siegel, Aki. 2022. Study abroad in Sweden: Japanese exchange students' perspectives of language use in university EMI courses. *Languages* 7 (1). https://doi.org/10.3390/languages7010003.

Stazicker, Anne, and Nancy Woods. 2022. *Teaching International Foundation Year: A practical guide for EAP practitioners in higher and further education.* London: Routledge.

Swain, Merrill, and Robert Keith Johnson. 1997. Immersion education: A category within bilingual education. In *Immersion education*, ed. Robert Keith Johnson and Merrill Swain, 1–16. Cambridge: Cambridge University Press.

Thornton, Margaret. 2011. *Privatising the public university*. Abingdon: Routledge.

Tibbetts, Neil Adam, and Timothy Chapman. 2023. *A guide to in-sessional English for academic purposes: Paradigms and practices*. New York: Routledge. https://doi.org/10.4324/9781003193715.

Universities UK. n.d. Specialist institutions. https://www.universitiesuk.ac.uk/what-we-do/supporting-our-members/specialist-institutions. Accessed 7 July 2025.

University of Cambridge. 2024. *About the university*. https://www.cam.ac.uk/about-the-university/history/early-records. Accessed 9 October 2024.

University of Edinburgh. 2024. *Hybrid learning and teaching*. https://institute-academic-development.ed.ac.uk/study-hub/learning-resources/hybrid-learning-and-teaching. Accessed 12 January 2025.

University of Hong Kong. 2024. *A transformative graduate curriculum*. https://tl.hku.hk/flexible-curriculum-structure/. Accessed 8 May 2024.

University of Nottingham Ningbo China. 2024. *Study with us*. https://www.nottingham.edu.cn/en/study-with-us/home.aspx. Accessed 14 October 2024.

Villegas, Paula. 2021. *Who wins when we flip? Exploring perceptions of flipped learning in an online EAP presessional course*. EdD thesis, University of Sheffield. https://etheses.whiterose.ac.uk/30849/.

Wake, Stephanie, Madeleine Pownall, Richard Harris, and Pam Birtill. 2023. Balancing pedagogical innovation with psychological safety? Student perceptions of authentic assessment. *Assessment and Evaluation in Higher Education* 49 (4): 511–522. https://doi.org/10.1080/02602938.2023.2275519.

Wallace, Susan. 2015. *A dictionary of education*, 2nd ed. Oxford: Oxford University Press.

Wiers-Jenssen, Jannecke. 2018. Paradoxical attraction? Why an increasing number of international students choose Norway. *Journal of Studies in International Education* 23 (2): 281–298. https://doi.org/10.1177/1028315318786449.

Wright, Clare, Anna Tsakalaki, and Mei Lin. 2022. "Now I hear what you say"—How short EAP courses can foster successful academic interactional strategies. *Journal of English for Academic Purposes* 55: 101074. https://doi.org/10.1016/j.jeap.2021.101074.

Xiaoqiong, Betsy Hu, and Jiang Xianxing. 2011. Kachru's Three Concentric Circles and English teaching fallacies in EFL and ESL contexts. *Changing English* 18 (2): 219–228. https://doi.org/10.1080/1358684X.2011.575254.

Yasuda, Sachiko. 2023. What does it mean to construct an argument in academic writing? A synthesis of English for general academic purposes and English for specific academic purposes. *Journal of English for Academic Purposes* 66: 101307. https://doi.org/10.1016/j.jeap.2023.101307.

4

The EAP Student

4.1 Raising Awareness of the EAP Student's Situation

The theme of this book is a humanistic approach to pedagogy in the discipline of EAP. This means that any pedagogical activities designed through this approach should be with the individual EAP learner in mind. For this reason, this chapter is dedicated to developing a learner profile of the EAP student to gain a better understanding of who they are and the journey they are undertaking. This chapter aims to raise awareness of the EAP student's journey and how this may impact on their EAP studies. Through reading and reflecting on my own work with learners, it is clear that each has their own individual journey, experiences and choices which impact on their EAP learning. This supports the motion for a humanistic approach. This chapter shows that the EAP student is different to a 'regular' academic studies student and that they may face additional struggles that may not be encountered by learners or other disciplines. This in turn can impact on their overall learning experience. In L1 English institutions, a regular student could be described as being one who is more likely to be classified as domestic and as a result studying a subject or subjects in a context that is likely to have some level of

L. Dyer, *A Humanistic Approach to English for Academic Purposes Pedagogy*, https://doi.org/10.1007/978-3-032-00186-3_4

familiarity to them. They are also not generally required to undertake a course of EAP study. This is in contrast to many non-L1 English students undertaking their studies in an L1 English context. These students are considered ready to undertake academic studies but are constrained through their English language proficiency attainment (Hu and Trenkic 2019) and as a result have a high probability of engaging in EAP studies. An EAP student is also more likely to be international or study in a context that could be considered international such as through TNE or EMI. Thus adaptation to that context may take more time than a domestic student in a domestic context. These additional factors have the potential to increase workload and/or time taken to complete work as the EAP student navigates studies alongside an array of other potential factors (see Sect. 4.6). Additionally, assumptions should not be made that all learners are the same with the same previous learning experiences (Kettle 2017; Akazaki 2010). In the UK, institutions offer comparable PSPs with similar learning outcomes that are accredited by similar professional organisations (Tibbetts and Chapman 2023). Nevertheless, the individual has their own path and a one size fits all approach to EAP might not prove to be fruitful. In order to delve more into the EAP student profile, this chapter is divided into the following sections. Firstly, it looks at emotions in EAP and why they are important to consider in the learning process. Next it looks at why learners study EAP before moving on to how they choose an EAP provider. Then, based upon the contexts reviewed in Chapter 3, it reflects on which students may study EAP in those situations. Finally it looks at barriers that may impact on an EAP student's learning. The factors reviewed are not an exhaustive list and there will be others not discussed in this publication.

4.2 Emotions in EAP

Section 1.3 showed that EAP can be split into three components:

A. Bridging the perceived language gap of what is considered a language deficit between completed studies and future studies in the English language

B. Raising consciousness and fostering the designated skills deemed necessary for academic study
C. Raising awareness of community skills

This threefold process has the potential to ignite a variety of emotions from the learner, at both positive and negative ends of the scale. Research has shown that emotions can be linked to academic achievement (Pekrun et al. 2017). Thus, being in an academic setting, an EAP learner's emotions can be influenced by their academic achievements. In an ideal scenario, EAP learners would maintain a positive psychological state throughout their course of study, but there many factors that could hold sway on their psychological equilibrium. By nature, EAP and PSPs in particular are intensive learning events which bring the student 'back to basics' in their learning process. It redirects the learner from the accumulation of knowledge to understanding how they learn to accumulate that knowledge. This pivot has the potential to unlock a variety of emotions. At the positive end are emotions such as determination, courage and strength (MacIntyre et al. 2019). These and other positive emotions have the potential to empower students and can be a predictor of positive outcomes (Wang et al. 2023), especially in relation to developing language (MacIntyre et al. 2019). In contrast, students who experience negative emotions such as boredom and hopelessness may make limited effort in their studies, affecting their overall outcomes (Wang et al. 2023). Additionally, should a student experience a negative situation in their studies over which they had no control, there is potential for them to move from the positive to the negative end of the scale (Seyri and Rezaee 2024). In the middle of the scale, students may also experience positive or negative deactivating emotions, in which they may participate in classroom activities but invest little time or effort and instead may prioritise other activities (Wang et al. 2023). In EAP, the increased workload of having to complete tasks in a language that is not a student's L1 has been shown to be a challenge for students. This opens the doors for potential negative emotions as students learn to manage this as does the linguistic complexities of understanding and producing work in English (Tatzl 2011). However, linguistic proficiency in the academic studies language of instruction has been shown to have a positive impact on academic success (Johnson 1988). Thus, as EAP is a support or precursor to academic studies, it has the potential to motivate and foster positive outcomes through the desire to achieve but the learner must be supported and be able to visualise these.

4.3 Why Do Learners Study EAP?

There are many reasons why learners may undertake a course in EAP such as preparing them to move from one educational context to another (British Council, n.d.). However, there are multiple factors behind this decision to study EAP which could be driven by both internal and external circumstances. This section looks at a selection of reasons why a learner may commit to a course of EAP study. This list covers many of what might be considered the most frequent reasons for EAP study. These reasons covered here are:

- Institutional English language proficiency requirements
- EAP is part of course requirements
- Requirement for visa or sponsor
- Needing extra support for academic studies
- Wanting extra support for academic studies
- Relevance for future plans.

4.3.1 Institutional English Language Proficiency Requirements

Many English language providers have entry language proficiency requirements in order to undertake their in-house studies. As a limited proficiency in English can impact upon success in academic studies, an institution may set a minimum English language proficiency level for students to obtain in order to proceed to direct entry to academic studies (Hu and Trenkic 2019). If a student does not meet the English language proficiency requirements, frequently determined by an English language testing system, they may be required to undertake a course of EAP study.

There are several English language testing systems available to learners such as IELTS, TOEFL, TOEIC and Pearson. These have become gate-keepers of linguistic capabilities for entry to many universities. In the UK, IELTS has been selected by the government as one of the methods of entry for international students to study in tertiary education (Pearson 2020a), which has resulted in students carrying out repeated test taking in order to achieve the necessary entry grade (Hu and Trenkic 2019). If a student achieves the required IELTS score for their desired programme of study, they are able to proceed directly to that program. In contrast, those who do not meet the direct entry requirements are likely to be required to undertake a course of EAP to bridge the gap between their IELTS score and the institutional entry requirements (Pearson 2020a). The distance between an applicant's IELTS score and institutional entry requirements frequently impact on the length of EAP study (Pearson 2020a). Thus those obtaining an IELTS score closer to the institutional entry requirements tend to be offered a shorter PSP than those who are further away (University of Leeds 2025).

4.3.2 EAP Is Part of Course Requirements

EAP may form a compulsory part of a course of study, such as for an IFP in the UK (NCUK 2024) or as a requirement for graduation (see Sect. 3.4.3). For entry to UK IFPs a student would normally have completed their secondary education outside the UK. Conditions may also apply for those who may have undertaken their previous education in English but in a different country to the intended institution. An example of this could be L1 English speakers from the USA wanting to do undergraduate study in the UK needing to complete an IFP and thus course integrated EAP study beforehand (NCUK, n.d.). Even if a student has completed their previous education in English, if study was in a location in which English is not the main language of communication, language test results are normally required to demonstrate proficiency (Charles and Pecorari 2015). This means that students who have previously studied in TNE or EMI contexts may also be required to undertake some form of EAP before commencing their academic studies. EAP may also be a study requirement within a university for all students, no matter what their field of study, and must be 'passed' in order to graduate (Zohoorian 2015).

4.3.3 Requirement for Visa or Sponsorship

Students may hold a particular visa or be a recipient of a particular scholarship which requires them to undertake a compulsory course of EAP as part of or a precursor to their academic studies. These requirements might range from a student undertaking a 6-week intensive module to a full year of EAP consisting of various modules signalling student progression. Students who fall into this category may already meet institutional entry requirements but are undertaking EAP to fulfil the needs of stakeholders (Jordan 1997).

4.3.4 Needing Extra Support for Academic Studies

Particularly applicable to ISPs, if a student is deemed to not be meeting the level of English or academic skills proficiency their academic department desires, they may be required or recommended to undertake additional EAP studies to support their disciplinary work (Tibbetts and Chapman 2023). ISPs may be offered on an optional or as compulsory basis. However, if an ISP is optional it may be seen as peripheral to academic studies (Sloan and Porter 2010) and thus a less attractive option for learners to attend.

4.3.5 Wanting Extra Support for Academic Studies

In addition to the external influences listed above, students could also have intrinsic reasons for studying EAP. One such example could be for the love of studying or the English language. In these instances the student may already meet the institutional English language entry requirements and could have chosen to proceed directly to their academic discipline. Additionally, a PSP may be used as a means for a learner to increase the length of their studies before embarking on their degree programmes.

4.3.6 Relevance for Future Plans

Students may choose to undertake EAP courses alongside their regular studies if they see it as beneficial to their academic studies and future careers (Liu et al. 2011; Evans and Green 2007).

4.4 Selecting an EAP Provider

This section examines a learner's selection of EAP provider. There are a range of factors that can influence a learner's selection of EAP provider. As with Sect. 4.3, this is not a complete list but includes what could be considered amongst the most common factors. Choosing an institution of EAP study may be determined by just one or many of the reasons below.

- **Reputation or quality of the course provider** (Espinoza et al. 2019; Cebolla-Boado et al. 2018; Bamford et al. 2006; Lin 1997 cited in Hu et al. 2022). Perceived levels of prestige can be significant in determining a student's choice of provider, especially if this may impact on future career prospects. As a result, institutions in this category have the potential to attract higher numbers of applications. This perceived prestige may be linked to the desired place of academic studies, to the EAP provider itself or both.
- **EAP provider's links with a specific academic studies provider** (Aspect International Language Academies 2024; Nuseir and El Refae 2022). In this context a student may choose a specific EAP provider due to their links with the potential academic studies institution. The availability of specific academic disciplines in one institution is one factor which may influence the EAP student to select an EAP provider who can provide access to that desired institution.

- **Institutional English language entry requirements** (Roche and Booth 2021). As shown in Sect. 4.3.1, entry requirements play a role in the institutional selection process and this in turn can determine an EAP provider's own entry requirements. For example, it is a given that entry requirements for a year-long PSP are lower than that of a short intensive course. Therefore, if a student does not meet the requirements to attend a short intensive course, they need to find a provider who offers the course they desire or need based on their current level of proficiency.
- **Proximity to home** (Hu et al. 2022; Nuseir and El Refae 2022). Proximity to home may also contribute to choosing an EAP provider. The increasing number of TNE and EMI educational providers increases the chance for learners to study closer to home if they so desire. On the other hand, students may wish to have a greater distance between their home and place of study, thus studying overseas may be an attractive choice.
- **Potential to study online** (Feubli et al. 2023; Marquis and Ghosh 2017) Students may prefer to study online if they find residence away from their regular domicile challenging or incompatible. Online study may also be preferred by part time students.
- **Facilities and extracurricular activities** (Nuseir and El Refae 2022) Institutional facilities and extracurricular activities can also play a role in determining student selection of provider. Facilities refer to factors such as sports amenities or libraries as well as the learning environment itself.
- **Tuition fees** (Nuseir and El Refae 2022; Luo and Jamieson-Drake 2015; Wakeling and Jefferies 2013). As mentioned in Sect. 3.2.1.3, tuition fees can vary by institution and its location. An institution which requests low or no tuition fee payment may be attractive for learners who are self-funding or have low budgets.
- **Living and additional study costs** (Francis and Franklin 2023). Coupled with tuition fees is living and additional study costs. If a location is viewed as being expensive it may be less attractive for learners with lower financial budgets.

- **Receipt of a scholarship or financial aid determining institution of study** (A.S. Hornby Educational Trust 2023). A student may have restrictions on or no choice in their place of study if it is predetermined by scholarship or financial aid provider.
- **Role of an external stakeholder such as a sponsor or agent** (Fittante 2023). A sponsor or agent may be involved in determining which institution a student attends through infrastructures that have been put in place. In this instance a student may have a choice of a limited number of institutions or no choice at all.
- **Personal links to the institution** (Pimpa 2005). Having a personal link to an educational provider, such as a family member having studied there, can influence a learner's decision in choosing their place of study.
- **Interest in the culture or locality of the institution** (Hu et al. 2022; Cebolla-Boado et al. 2018). This too can influence a learner's choice of institution, with learner's wishing to experience different cultures alongside their learning.

4.5 Who Is the EAP Student?

The following sections focus on a key aspect of this publication—determining who the EAP student is. It is through this profile that it will be shown that the EAP student is 'different' from a regular academic studies student and that a more compassionate approach should be taken to in recognition of this.

Whilst it may be impossible to draw up one single overarching profile of the EAP student, something which is true for all is that no EAP student is a beginner in the English language. That is to say that all EAP students will have gone through some form of acquisition of the English language prior to their EAP studies such as general English lessons, L1 English language acquisition or immersion through educational programmes. It can therefore be said that the EAP student already has the preparatory language skills to progress to EAP study.

This section uses the contexts presented in Chapter 3 to discover who the EAP student is. From these contexts, it is clear that the EAP student may have many profiles and that students do not simply fit into one but rather multiple contexts. For example an EAP student may be one of the following:

- Studying EAP on a full time EGAP PSP for one academic year in an inner circle institution for entry to undergraduate study in that institution
- Studying EAP an ESAP ISP for two semesters in TNE context to support taught postgraduate academic studies
- Undertaking a non-credit bearing compulsory EGAP course in an outer circle institution as a requirement for graduation

As with Chapter 3, the contexts in this section are separated into four main sections, each with subdivisions. These are

- Physical contexts
- Geographical location of the learning institution
- Institution type
- Content contexts
- Level
- Specificity
- Construct contexts
- Timeliness
- Mode
- Value
- Duration
- Demographic contexts
- Cohort language
- Cohort nationality
- The role of the teacher

4.5.1 Physical Contexts

Physical contexts cover the geographical location of the learning institution and the institution type. Both of these physical contexts can play a role in determining student profile.

4.5.1.1 Geographical Location of Learning Institution

As shown in Sect. 3.2.1, the global expansion of EAP means that whereas once the EAP student may only have been classed as international, its expansion means that there is a growing number of domestic EAP students. In HE, a student can be described as international if they cross an international border in order to undertake educational activities, with around 6.4 million students worldwide meeting this definition in 2021 (Global Migration Data Portal 2024). In the majority of instances, an international student would be required to relocate to the educational host country in order to undertake their studies. In the past, many of these students would have relocated to an inner circle location. However, the spread of EAP means students may commute to their place of study by crossing an international border, which can also enable them to be called international students. One such example of this is the daily movement of students from Malaysia to Singapore (Hutchinson et al. 2023). Singapore has become a hub for outer circle EAP, with governmental policies aiming to increase international student numbers (Chacko 2020) and thus an increasing provision of EAP. EAP students in the outer circle may have been educated through the medium of English, may use English as the main means of communication or indeed have had little exposure to the language. The outer circle is an expanding market with increasing numbers choosing to undertake study in those nations as opposed the inner circle (Kobayashi 2011). In addition to the physical movement of students, an online student may also be deemed as international as they cross a virtual international border to undertake their studies (Kang and Chang 2016). The expanding circle too continues to be a major area of growth for EAP. In these locations the student profile is most likely to be made up of a majority of non-L1 English speakers

(Charles and Pecorari 2015) who could be classified as international or domestic. A domestic student can be classified as either residential or commuter. Residential students relocate to the vicinity of the educational provider in order to undertake studies there and commuter students remain at their ordinary place of residence but commute to the institution for studies during term time (Hallam 2023). With the increasing number of inner circle institution satellite campuses and the growth of EAP in both the outer and expanding circle, there is now an increasing likelihood that the EAP student can be classified as both domestic and commuter.

4.5.1.2 Institution Type

As highlighted in Sect. 3.2.2, there are no clear definitions for both public and private universities. For public universities there is a common narrative that they strive for an image of prestige. This leads to highly selective admissions processes which can restrict access to the institution to those who may be considered elite (Orphan 2020). Being considered a prestigious institution can generate more power in terms of sector influence, financial donations and applicant numbers (Taylor and Cantwell 2019). As such the English language proficiency entry requirements for these universities may reflect entry requirement for academic studies. Thus, institutions with high level entry requirements for academic studies may also have high entry requirements for EAP.

In contrast to public institutions, private institutions may seek alternative ways to attract students. This could be through emphasising the perceived quality of its academic and infrastructural credentials alongside its ability to adapt to a changing educational market for more learning personalisation (Husain et al. 2018). However, there may be financial challenges for students to attend these institutions as there may be no government grant or funding available (Meyer and Schreiber 2024). As a result there may be fewer students from low-income backgrounds attending private universities.

Students attending a specialist institution are likely to need to demonstrate their existing skillset in the institution's discipline, show their potential capabilities through academic achievement either through previous study or entry examination (Royal College of Music 2025) or meet specific personal criteria as having a military role (Le et al. 2017). Being a specialist, there is more chance that the learner has experienced positive achievement emotions (see Sect. 2.6.2.5) and hence has a higher level of motivation for their discipline.

4.5.2 Content Contexts

Content contexts can play a significant role in determining the EAP student profile. For example, if a prospective student is hoping to undertake postgraduate research in a specific academic discipline then a provider who can offer EAP at a postgraduate level and in that area, this would likely appear more attractive than a single EGAP course which caters for all students at all levels.

4.5.2.1 Level

As previously highlighted, EAP can take place at any educational level from compulsory schooling to postgraduate research. However, it is clear that HE is the most common setting for EAP is at the three levels of tertiary education: undergraduate, taught postgraduate and research postgraduate. In order for a student to undertake EAP for entry to undergraduate level, they would normally be expected to have completed secondary level education. The age group for this level is likely to be around 18 years though students may be accepted at a younger or older age and may also be classified as a mature student. For entry to taught postgraduate study, it is normally expected that students would have completed undergraduate study. Students undertaking EAP for entry to taught postgraduate study may progress directly from their undergraduate degree or come to EAP after a gap following study. It is therefore expected that the EAP student at this stage is above the age of 18, most likely being in their early 20s at the youngest. Entry requirements for entry to research postgraduate may vary from institution, with some allowing entry direct from undergraduate study and others requiring a taught postgraduate qualification. As with entry to taught postgraduate study, students may progress directly from their previous degree or re-enter education following a gap. However, as with students intending to undertake taught postgraduate study, research postgraduates are also likely to be in their early 20s or above. Being more 'mature', postgraduate learners are often more goal-orientated than their younger counterparts and are able to relate their contemporary learning experiences to learning goals. They are also more likely to have higher levels of intrinsic motivation (Sanderson Cole 2012) which could have positive impacts on their EAP learning experience.

4.5.2.2 Specificity

Section 3.3.2 highlighted the increasing divergence of EAP into the strands of EGAP to ESAP. Whilst some institutions may have a variety of ESAP programmes in place, others may maintain the EGAP approach or perhaps mix EGAP with some ESAP. Being the 'original' form of EAP, EGAP is the mainstream approach and more widely taught than ESAP (Li and Heron 2021). Institutions may choose to offer EGAP to all before learners are separated into discipline specific strands (University of Hong Kong 2024; University of Leeds 2025). Although it may be considered that students of some academic disciplines would benefit from ESAP, student demand, due to factors such as external examinations, may influence institutions and students themselves to undertake EGAP study (Li and Heron 2021). Learners may also value EGAP as that foundation to set them on their academic pathways (Gaffas 2019) rather than ESAP which could be considered more challenging.

ESAP provides learners with a curriculum more tailored to their future academic discipline. Thus it could serve as a motivator and it could be argued that ESAP learners will have some interest in their future disciplinary studies. As a result they may take a positive approach to their ESAP learning as they visualise themselves in their future ideal self. However, ESAP does raise issues with an example of this being when students become increasingly focused on the EAP-ness of their work. This action can be detrimental to the academic output they are required to produce. Examples of this could include the overuse of signposting discourse and students learning specific referencing styles by heart at the expense of content and criticality. Reasons for this focus on EAP, which I call the 'EAP bubble', rather than academic content could be due to student familiarity with or the safety net of EAP or disengagement with their discipline. Subsequently, although a student is often considered successful in EAP if they are able to transfer their acquired knowledge and skills to their academic studies, the impact of too much EAP in academic work could potentially be damaging to eventual outcomes.

4.5.3 Construct Contexts

The following contexts may influence student profile as it is these factors can influence student choices in their selection of an EAP provider.

4.5.3.1 Timeliness

The separation of EAP provision into PSP and ISP can provide the students with a contrasting learning experience. The student profile in both contexts differs in that PSPs are to be taken prior to academic studies and ISP as support during. In a PSP it is the norm for EAP to be the sole overarching focus of the learner's studies for the duration of the course (Alexander et al. 2019). The learner is provided with the environment to become immersed in the requirements and outputs of the course. Whilst the PSP allows for the student to develop the skills that can be taken forward to their academic studies, a potential EAP bubble may have negative impacts (see Sect. 4.5.2.2). Such examples of this include that it may provide the learner with learning conditions that are not replicated in their academic studies such as small class sizes and regular teacher support. A further component of the EAP bubble is the role of peers. Peer support, be it academic or emotional, may be more readily available in a PSP as students have the opportunity to bond with others that they see repeatedly over the course duration. In contrast, in academic studies students may find themselves more isolated as they leave their EAP support network and move into disciplinary work. This is particularly the case for research postgraduates, who due to the nature of their studies, may find themselves at risk of loneliness (Harrison et al. 2023).

In contrast, ISPs may have more haphazard student attendance, perhaps caused by students placing more effort on their academic studies, timetabling clashes or their own time management. Additionally, as ISPs are generally only allocated to non-L1 speakers of English, they could be viewed by those learners that they are in deficit to L1 speakers and isolates them from other students (Tibbetts and Chapman 2023). This could result in the ISP being considered less attractive to students.

4.5.3.2 Mode

Mode can play a significant role in shaping the EAP student profile. The increasing changes in course delivery type alongside institutional eagerness to attract students mean that offering a variety of study options is becoming more commonplace. Despite developments in technology enabling other methods of study, the traditional approach to teaching and learning, face-to-face in a classroom, remains a popular choice for learners. As highlighted in Sect. 3.2.1, many nations are looking to increase their international student enrolments and thus increase potential on campus EAP provision. This means that face-to-face learning will continue to be a popular choice for learners. Many, or indeed the majority, of these will be studying full time meaning that EAP is their sole educational focus. In contrast to face-to-face learning, in an online context it is unlikely that the student would be required to spend the same amount of time in an online lesson as they would in a physical classroom situation. Thus, even though an online EAP course may be classed as full time, in reality the learner has a more flexible learning schedule due to the restricted live time with the teacher and an extensive time allocated for independent study (Arias et al. 2018). Timetabled independent study may in reality be work or family time, with the learner rescheduling their independent study for a time more suited to their needs. Due to online learning's independent nature, it is expected that students who undertake this mode should have positive attitude towards this construct (Guo et al. 2014) and expect that they will be self-driven in their learning (Binali et al. 2021). A mixed online and face-to-face programme has also been shown as having a positive impact on EAP learners as they demonstrate higher levels of engagement and attainment through the two different learning contexts (Monika and V 2022). In terms of part time learning the availability of part time EAP PSP provision is significantly less than full time, likely due to a number of reasons such as visa requirements, age of applicant or institutions simply not offering part time options. A learner's decision to undertake study on a part time basis could be influenced by a number of factors such as finances, personal circumstances or to undertake other activities such as employment (Bennion et al. 2011). On the other hand, as an ISP is concurrent support for academic studies it can only be taken on a part time basis.

4.5.3.3 Value

Value placed on a course of EAP can influence the student profile. Taking into account credit bearing EAP, these courses may be compulsory for students on specific programmes only or as credit for part of academic studies. Such EAP courses have been shown to have a positive impact on both student engagement and higher GPAs than students who did not take them (Fenton-Smith et al. 2018). Credit bearing EAP courses can take place alongside or before academic studies and are more likely to take the form of ESAP (see Sect. 3.3.2.2) (Fenton-Smith et al. 2015). There is the question of which students should take the course can prove challenging and may meet with resistance should it be implemented for all, including domestic L1 English speakers (Fenton-Smith et al. 2015). For compulsory but not credit bearing modules or preparatory gatekeeping courses a variety of profiles have been identified. For example students may demonstrate high levels of engagement and motivation as they realise the need to pass the class to achieve their desired learning outcomes (Ataç et al. 2018; Miller et al. 2021). Even those with high command of English have been shown to value the usefulness of compulsory EAP provision (Yung and Fong 2019). However, students may feel unhappy due being required to undertake EAP because they wish to focus their time on their academic studies instead (Ataç et al. 2018). In terms of optional EAP, research has shown that students in this context are more likely to achieve higher grades than those on compulsory courses due to higher levels of motivation and engagement (Ataç et al. 2018). Yet due to its optional nature, learners may feel less responsibility for completing tasks and there may be less regular attendance due to lack of requirements (Ataç et al. 2018).

4.5.3.4 Duration

The duration of an EAP programme also has the potential to play a role in the EAP student profile. Regarding PSPs it is generally a given that students with a level of English language proficiency far from a HE provider's entry requirements would undertake a longer course of EAP study than those students whose proficiency level is closer (University of Leeds 2025; University of Nottingham 2025). Using IELTS scores as an example, if one institution requires a 7.0 proficiency for entry to their academic studies, a student with a score of 6.5 would likely need to attend a shorter PSP than a student with a score of 6.0. In contrast, a student with an IELTS score of 5.0 will likely be required to undertake a significantly longer course of EAP. Due to this lower entry score, students undertaking a longer course of EAP may have a higher level of needs than those on short courses. This is because short intensive EAP courses are often used by institutions to bridge negligible perceived linguistic deficits (Pearson 2020a) which at lower scoring levels could be deemed more significant. However, external factors may also influence the length of study such as requirements put in place by stakeholders. These can determine that even if a student is relatively close to proficiency entry requirements they still should undertake an extended EAP study. In contrast the PSP student, an ISP student is already deemed to have achieved the required linguistic proficiencies needed to carry out academic study through the medium of English. However, what the ISP does is provide an intervention to enable that student to succeed in their learning (Tibbetts and Chapman 2023). In an Anglophone setting, and

ISP may have varying lengths, perhaps covering one or two semesters of an undergraduate degree for example. However, in an EMI setting there is a likelihood that ISP provision is ongoing throughout academic studies, with the potential for it to be credit bearing and a requirement for graduation (University of Hong Kong 2024). It may also be taken by an entire cohort (Tibbetts and Chapman 2023) rather than those who are regarded as needing extra support.

4.5.4 Demographic Contexts

As stated in Chapter 3, these contexts could be considered pertinent in determining who the EAP student is as it considers personal designation and characteristics—nationality and language. The teacher too can play a significant role in shaping a student's profile.

4.5.4.1 Cohort Language

A monolingual cohort may be made up of a single or multiple nationalities. The commonality in L1 may lead to translanguaging amongst learners which could be viewed as a help as communication is facilitated (Lewis et al. 2012; Alkhateeb 2018), especially if the L1 is considered close to English (Ortega-Llebaria and Colantoni 2014). However, this may also lead to negative effects (Kazazoglu 2020) which can create challenges different to those students whose L1 may be further from English. Translanguaging may also be a hindrance where the L1 becomes a space psychological safety (Dryden et al. 2021) where learners can communicate without fear of being judged on their comments in English. However, even if translanguaging may be accepted in certain contexts, students may choose to translanguaging for finetuning their work yet work through the medium of English for the majority of their efforts (Tastanbek 2024). Translanguaging also allows for the learner to obtain a more in-depth understanding of their target language which they may not be able to achieve solely through monolingualism. It can also prove to be motivating for those learners who may be struggling with the target language, with translanguaging serving as a scaffolding process to achieving target language requirements (Masoudi 2025).

As with a monolingual cohort, a multilingual cohort might consist of a single or multiple nationalities, with English being the unifying means of communication. A cohort can be considered multilingual even if there is just a single student whose L1 differs from the L1 which may be shared by all of the remaining students. Should the cohort consist of multiple L1s, it is more likely that English will be the sole language of communication between learners. However, in the situation where one L1 dominates, these students may resort to translanguaging, thus alienating learners who do not speak the same language and leading to feelings of intolerance (Kim et al. 2014).

4.5.4.2 Cohort Nationality

The student profile in this context shares traits with that of cohort language. If students are of the same nationality and they are domestic students, they are more likely to be familiar with the educational norms and practices in their country of study. Thus teaching and learning approaches in EAP may continue as such. In contrast, if a single nationality group consists entirely of an 'international' nationality, then educators need to be aware of the academic cultural differences and the process of adaptation the students need to progress through on their educational pathway (Tian and Lowe 2013). In a mixed nationality group there is potential for exploring and intercultural understanding. However, as with cohort language, if the mixed nationality group consists of one student of a specific nationality with all remaining students of another, there is potential for isolation for those learners as suggested in Sect. 4.5.4.1. Whilst research has shown that international students generally have a more positive demeanour in EAP teaching and learning (Kim et al. 2014; Chapple 2015; Wilang and Nupong 2022), by simply being 'international' those students have additional pathways to navigate which have potential to interrupt the learning process (see Sect. 4.6).

4.5.4.3 The Role of the Teacher

There are many ways in which the teacher may influence the profile of the EAP student, in both positive and negative respects. One potential impact to mention is boredom. Boredom occurs when an activity is perceived as has having a low sense of value and there is no control sense of control over the learning process, giving an overall feeling of dissatisfaction (Acee et al. 2010). Research has shown EAP students may experience boredom through teacher control—either too much or too little (Li et al. 2021), perceived meaningless tasks (Li et al. 2021) and repetitive activities which in turn leads to disengagement (Pawlak et al. 2020) and consequently lower academic attainment (Mousavian Rad et al. 2022). These situations could be considered a counter-humanistic approach to pedagogy as they contradict the concepts of autonomy, authenticity and acculturation put forward by Aloni (see Sect. 2.6.2.2) as well as Rogers' student-centred learning (see Sect. 2.6.1.3), Maslow's peak experience (see Sect. 2.6.1.2) and Montessori's role of curiosity in learning (Sect. 2.6.1.1). These can all act as barriers to flow (see Sect. 2.6.2.3), affect motivation levels (Sect. 2.6.2.4) and lead to the rise of negative emotions (see Sects. 2.6.2.1, 2.6.2.5, 2.6.2.6). Feelings of detachment from or not understanding the value of tasks can have negative impacts on studies (Zawodniak et al. 2021), affecting the potential for sustainable learning (see Sect. 2.6.2.8). As EAP originates in a Western context, it applies the Western style of power relations where the teacher is not the sole authority in the classroom (Zhang 2021). A Western style student-centred pedagogy shifts the learner from a teacher focused to a student-centred learning experience. Consequently, students with limited experience of this style of teaching may find it challenging to adapt (Zhang 2021) which could lead to instances of boredom. It has been suggested that inclusivity process and procedures should also be applied to international students to promote a better sense of belonging (Bai and Wang 2022) in order to avoid intersectionality processes through being potentially both international and a non-L1 English speaker. Thus changes to pedagogical practices could aid in providing a less boredom inducing learning environment which is aware of the multiple challenges that EAP learners may face.

4.6 Factors That May Impact on EAP Study

This section looks at factors that may impact on the EAP student's learning experience. Whilst 'regular' students face challenges in their academic studies, EAP students may encounter more barriers to their learning due to a range of factors such as whether learners undertake their studies abroad in a physical or contextual sense. In this case there may be a period of adjustment to both the academic and personal domains (Beaven and Spencer-Oatey 2016), alongside contemplating rhetoric, discourse and academic conventions which could be in contrast to or challenge their previous learning experiences (Akazaki 2010). Understanding the experiences of students is important in the creating of academic programmes (Sümer et al. 2008). These factors may impact on EAP study through restriction, distraction or confusion. These factors may impact the student in a way that could be considered mild, moderate or significant. One single factor that has a significant impact on the student could lead to serious interruption to the learning process. Alternatively a combination of factors with mild impact could also have a significant affect on a student's learning. Each of the factors reviewed in this section can be considered as having a potentially detrimental impact on the learning experience. This is not a complete list of all factors that can affect EAP students (or indeed any student) and there may of course be others that can impact on student learning. The issues outlined in this section are:

- Red tape
- Social culture shock
- Financial and lifestyle factors
- Caring responsibilities
- Trauma and crises
- Language shock
- Academic culture shock
- Digitality
- Inclusivity
- The role of stakeholders

4.6.1 Red Tape

Defined as being 'official rules and processes that seem unnecessary and delay results' (Cambridge Dictionary 2024), red tape has the potential to play a significant role in the student learning experience. Bureaucratic difficulties surrounding issues such as administration, financial support, visa regulations and permits can all lead to detrimental results in student participation and eventual course outcome. These negative experiences can affect a learner's sense of belonging and feelings of success in their educational experience (Reeves 2015). Some examples of red tape that may effect student learning include:

- Delays in tuition fee payment from sponsor or other external organisation, leading to either temporary (until fees are paid) or permanent withdrawal of the student from the course. This can impact on the ability for the student to submit work as well as being unable to attend lessons and access learning materials. This has meant that when the tuition fees are eventually paid, the student finds themselves at a disadvantage, making them time poor and playing catch up, causing stress and pressure.
- Delays with residency permits or other official documentation. This may lead to the requirement for students to attend various administrative processes meetings to confirm their participation and attendance at their host institution. Compulsory appointments could take place during teaching and learning hours, affecting attendance and participation. In addition, stress caused by the issue can cause distraction and fatigue for those affected, impacting on their academic performance.

4.6.2 Social Culture Shock

Social culture shock can be described as the emotional disorientation a person feels when experiencing a new culture. In this section, the term social culture shock is used to differentiate it from the other culture shocks discussed in this chapter—namely language (Sect. 4.6.6) and academic (Sect. 4.6.7). Although it is expected that social culture shock is more likely to happen when moving from one nation to another, it can also occur when moving from one region to another within a nation (Kiziltas 2022). This means there is the potential for social culture shock to arise not only in those EAP students who choose to study abroad but also in those who may relocate to an institution in another region within their own country. Whilst studying abroad is viewed on the whole as being a positive and defining experience for individuals (Dall'Alba and Sidhu 2013), it has been shown to also have negative impacts on mental health (Minami et al. 2021), especially when less satisfying outcomes can also occur (Jæger and Gram 2019). International students may experience social culture shock in their destination country, with those affected more likely to have a lower quality of life satisfaction which in turn can impact on their academic studies (Presbitero 2016; Sherry et al. 2010). Ward et al.'s (2005) ABC model identifies three components of social culture shock—Affect, Behaviours and Cognitions. The affective component refers to the stresses one goes through in moving to an unfamiliar location. Behaviours considers the difficulties one may experience in adjusting to the new location. Cognition relates to the perception of oneself and place in society in the new location. Navigating the stages of the ABC model could be time consuming and distracting for a learner who is executing these tasks alongside EAP study and possibly other non-academic factors.

4.6.3 Financial and Lifestyle Factors

As shown in Chapter 3, there is discordance between whether or not an educational provider charges tuition fees and undertaking a course of EAP may add to a student's study costs. For fee paying institutions there may be additional tuition fees to cover the cost of a PSP on top of subsequent academic studies tuition fees. Additionally, being domiciled away from home can further increase costs to cover any rental and living expenses. For some learners from less affluent backgrounds, a scheme of financial support may be put in place to enable their studies and living costs (Lewine et al. 2022; Soar et al. 2022). However, others who do not meet the requirements or do not apply for support may find themselves fall into financial hardship and undertake activities which may have an impact on their studies. One approach that students may take to dealing with financial hardship is undertaking part time work (Newton and Turale 2000), which in turn can impact on student success through increased fatigue and distractions from academic life.

A further factor that can impact on the learning experience is accommodation. Research suggests that the financial stresses and habitation of substandard accommodation has a detrimental impact on the experience of international students (Hassan et al. 2023). Student issues with accommodation may relate to its condition, landlord relationship, roommate relationship (Gbadegesin et al. 2021) as well as neighbourhood safety and access to public transport (Zasina and Antczak 2023). All of these aspects have the potential to influence the EAP student profile and hence their EAP studies.

4.6.4 Caring Responsibilities

Students with caring responsibilities, such as those with dependent children, often view themselves positively as role models for their dependents both financially, academically (Navarro-Cruz et al. 2023) and in employment status (Brooks 2015). As a result, these learners may be highly motivated in their studies. If the learner is in a familiar location for the duration of their studies, such as in their home region, the impact of caring for others may have less of an impact than those who take up residence in a new location. If the learner studies away from home and brings their dependents with them, childcare or schooling may be needed (Navarro-Cruz et al. 2023). In this situation, the learner would need familiarise themselves with childcare or schooling processes in this new location. This could impact on learners in several ways:

1. Financially if fees are involved for the childcare or schooling. As a result, parents may choose to undertake some form of employment alongside their studies (Navarro-Cruz et al. 2023).

2. Taking up time as the parent organises appropriate childcare or schooling. Time may also be taken up if emergency care for a child is needed which in turn could impact on student attendance and ability to complete course tasks (Navarro-Cruz et al. 2023).
3. Taking up time and finances to find suitable healthcare providers (Doyle et al. 2016).

Support networks may weaken if others who provided support, such as other family members, remain behind in the home location (Brooks 2015). This increases self-reliance and can lead to isolation and difficulties adapting to the new situation (Brooks 2015).

4.6.5 Trauma and Crises

Trauma and crises can too affect learning experiences. There are numerous situations that could be classed as trauma and crises, but this section focuses on one and that is the displaced student. These students may fall into multiple categories such as refugee, asylum seeker, leave to remain in their current domain or other form of sanctuary (University of Leicester, no date). It has been highlighted that many students in these categories may find academic studies overwhelming as they adjust to their new normal. They may also have difficulties in accessing HE as they struggle to evidence previous educational attainments (Stevenson and Baker 2018 cited by McKenna and Palanac 2025). Issues may also be caused by financial constraints, with PSPs in particular often charging high tuition fees (Pearson 2020b). Yet despite these barriers, many students from these backgrounds have a strong desire to be successful in university work for both themselves and their families (Anderson 2020). In spite of the complexities they face both academically and in non-academic life, education is a controlling and supporting constituent that can bring about hope and a new focus (Lenette 2016). But for many displaced students it is language and literacy that can act as a barrier to learning, highlighting the need for support in these areas. Concurrently, there is also a gender imbalance in displaced student enrolment with enrolments being male dominated (Anderson 2020), highlighting potential further barriers. Issues noted by refugee students was the feeling of being treated as though they were of a lower language level than they actually were (Wilson et al. 2022) and not being challenged in their EAP learning due to being treated as 'victims' (Shakya et al. 2010 cited by Wilson et al. 2022). Education can return the student to their previous life which has been disrupted by events beyond their control (Wilson et al. 2022) but by labelling a student as a 'victim' there is the potential for them not to be treated the same as others.

4.6.6 Language Shock

Language shock is defined as distress from disorientation which results from inability to understand or to communicate in the language of the host environment (Schumann 1975 cited in Bai and Wang 2022). This can affect learners at any level, from those who have limited (Foreman 2003 cited in Bai and Wang 2022) to those with proficient levels of language (Marr 2005 cited in Bai and Wang 2022). Although students may be considered successful learners of English in their home country, they are often unprepared and confused by the Englishes they encounter in their study destination. This is because they may not only have to demonstrate ability to communicate in English but also adhere to the norms of academic discourse (Drennan 2022) which may vary geographically. Both Bai and Wang (2022) and Marr (2005) point to learners experiencing language shock, influenced by limited language awareness and misconceptions around accent dialect and 'standard' English (Marr 2005). This in turn becomes a barrier which can impact on a learner's ability to gather information, both academically and in everyday situations (Huang et al. 2011; Sherry et al. 2010), potentially slowing down and/or increasing workload in the learning process.

4.6.7 Academic Culture Shock

As with social culture shock and language culture shock, learners may experience an academic culture shock as they encounter an academic environment that may be different from what they have previously experienced. Studying away from one's home academic culture may require time to adapt as the learner moves to an educational system which contrasts to previous experiences (Sherry et al. 2010). Being 'away' refers to the physical distance of an institution from a student's domicile or previous educational experience. Even by studying online or at an inner circle institution satellite campus in their home location, students could still be 'away' when living in their regular domicile if the academic culture is of significant contrast to earlier studies. There are multiple factors which may cause a student to experience academic culture shock, but for this section only two are touched on: assessment and transition through educational stages.

4.6.7.1 Assessment

One example of academic culture shock is methods of assessment. For instance, one academic culture's norm may be to use exams (Zhang 2021) but another might favour the use of coursework. Whilst the majority of examinations require students to be assessed through writing, coursework can assess other areas such as fieldwork, artwork and dissertations (Heywood 2000 cited in Bridges et al. 2002). In general, it has been noted that the use of coursework or exam plus coursework yields higher grades than exams alone (Richardson 2014). However, the choice of assessment type varies across disciplines with STEM disciplines more likely to use exam based assessment (Lipnevich et al. 2020). In terms of EAP there is a clear trend for coursework-based assessment as students demonstrate their gradual acquisition of academic language and skills. It is unlikely that an EAP course will have a laboratory experiment as part of its assessment makeup but it is highly likely that it will be more coursework rather than exam focused. This could be problematic for those learners coming from an exam driven educational background (Ro 2019). Thus for those students moving to EAP from a contrasting previous educational experience, there is potential for interruption to learning as they attempt to navigate through the assessment barriers.

4.6.7.2 Transition Through Educational Stages and Phases

There is no doubt that there is a significant step in moving from secondary to tertiary level education systems. Students may find themselves dealing with a change in learning style from dependent to independent alongside developing personal and financial independence (UCAS 2024; Juma et al. 2016). Those who are considered more independent learners adapt more quickly to the demands of change of educational experience placed on them than dependent learners (Christie et al. 2013). Developing independent learning skills can be challenging for all learners. Yet university in the UK is based upon the exemplar of the independent learner (Christie et al. 2013) meaning that those who do not fit that profile may find it challenging to succeed. Input sessions in higher education may also differ from the school experience, with universities frequently using a mixture of large-scale lectures, small group seminars (UCAS 2024) and one-to-one discussions with lecturers or likewise. This could be a challenge for learners to adapt to as the teacher is removed from the figure of authority in the learning process.

A further rung on the educational ladder is the one where the learner transitions from undergraduate to postgraduate study. Master's study, whilst being at a higher level than undergraduate, may prove to be as big a step as the one from secondary to undergraduate level (Newcastle University 2025). That said, taught postgraduate study is generally completed at a more intensive rate than undergraduate (in one to two years as opposed to three to five) and involves more learner independence, in depth analysis and understanding (Newcastle University 2025). Critical thinking is often the key indicator in defining the difference between undergraduate and postgraduate study (Watson and Reissner 2010 cited in Evans et al. 2018) and as a result students may feel isolated (Armstrong 2009 cited in Evans et al. 2018) or like a 'fresher' again (Gibney et al. 2011) as they negotiate the new learning processes. Learners moving to postgraduate study are often considered to already possess the skills and confidence to undertake study due to their age and having already completed undergraduate studies (White 2023). However, whilst many students enter postgraduate study with a realisation of what is required of them academically, they may struggle to adapt and appear underprepared for academic independence and application of criticality (Evans et al. 2018). For the EAP student, digitality could act as a further barrier to the learning process.

4.6.8 Digitality

Digitality, be it through digital transformation or the teaching of digital skills, has become an integral part of education and it is now expected that institutions function through some form of digital media. As technology develops, universities are facing the increasing challenge to adopt and adapt to new digitality. However, within in these trends, universities retain inflexible systems (Butcher and Curry 2022) meaning that if a student is unable to adapt to a digitally enhanced learning system, they face falling behind or even ceasing their studies. Students with the most limited digital literacy skills face the challenge of learning not only discipline for their studies but also digital literacy skills, which can be time consuming, costly and stressful. This presents an obstacle to participation which can impact negatively on the eventual outcome of a learner's studies (Butcher and Curry 2022).

Alongside digital literacy is digital poverty. Defined by the Digital Poverty Alliance (2024) as 'the inability to interact with the online world fully, when, where, and how an individual needs to', digital poverty can impact on a learner's potential to embrace all opportunities available to them in a learning context. Technology comes at a cost and learners may need to borrow equipment from their institution to carry out their studies. Learners in this situation may find themselves at a further disadvantage if they require training to aid their digital literacy. Further issues can occur when there is not sufficient equipment available for those who need it, thus impacting on participation.

4.6.9 Inclusivity

Inclusivity refers to providing those who may feel marginalised with access to the same resources and opportunities as those who can be considered as non-marginalised. For this section, inclusivity is addressed in relation to disabled students. As an educational market expands, the number of disabled students also increases (Universities Australia 2019 cited by Edwards 2022). However, a relatively high number of students choose not to disclose disability to their university (Edwards 2022). Stigma is one of the most significant reasons for the non-disclosure and more visible disabilities being more likely to be disclosed than hidden disabilities (Clark et al. 2018). Students who do not disclose their disability to their university may not receive the same support for their learning from their institution which could leave them at a disadvantage in their studies. For a student to have adjustments made to their education, the institution must determine if the adjustment could be considered as appropriate for all those involved which includes the student, educators and other services such as the library. The institution may decide to apply or reject the adjustment request (Edwards 2022). For those who receive adjustments, there may be time delay as adjustments are put in place. For those whose adjustment requests are rejected, there are also potential delays as the learner may require time or support to manage their studies. One specific learning difference that may be diagnosed in later life or may not be picked up on non-English language contexts is dyslexia. As a phoneme complex language, English has been shown to have a higher rate of dyslexics than other languages (Ziegler et al. 2003). Therefore, it is possible some learners of EAP may not have been aware they were dyslexic until undertaking English language studies. The process from receiving a diagnosis to the implementation of reasonable adjustments in the learning environment can be a lengthy process and have the potential to cause interruption to the learning process.

4.6.10 The Role of Stakeholders

A stakeholder can be described as being any person, persons or organisation with an interest in another's activities (Law 2009). In education the stakeholder is an external party with the student being the recipient of the interest. External parties or stakeholders involved in education can include family (Pimpa 2005) and educators alongside governments, educational institutions, corporations and private foundations who may hold a vested interest through the form of student scholarships (Campbell and Neff 2020). For example, due to the limited amount of scholarships available, applicants or nominees are often required to meet certain criteria to be a recipient. The selection process may be based on various criteria such as family income, family status, housing status, academic achievement (Akilli and Cetin 2020) and nationality (Latief and Lin 2018). The resulting scholarship may then require the student to meet some form of expectation and impact (Gašević et al. 2022) such as through obtaining specific academic targets or facilitate cultural understanding (Latief and Lin 2018) which has the potential to increase both academic and non-academic workload.

4.7 Concluding the EAP Student

As with most learners, EAP students face a variety of challenges when undertaking their studies. However, EAP students may face additional challenges which can be influenced by a range of factors. This chapter has looked emotions involved in EAP and their potential impact. It has examined reasons why learners may undertake EAP studies, which are driven by both internal and external factors. It has also presented profiles of who the EAP student may be using the contexts presented in Chapter 3 as a framework. It has demonstrated that the EAP student profile is drawn from multiple contexts. Finally, this chapter has considered factors that may impact on the EAP student's learning experience. These factors could be influenced by the contexts in which EAP is being studied as well as other external determinants. All of this highlights the need for care and consideration in the designing of EAP courses as learners navigate a host of pathways to achieve their desired outcomes.

References

Acee, Taylor W., Hyunjin Kim, Hyunjin Kim, Jung-In Kim, Hsiang-Nin R. Chu, Myoungsook Kim, YoonJung Cho and Frank W. 2010. Academic boredom in under- and over-challenging situations. *Contemporary educational psychology* 35 (1): 17–27. https://doi.org/10.1016/j.cedpsych.2009.08.002.

A.S. Hornby Educational Trust. 2023. A.S. Hornby Educational Trust. https://www.hornby-trust.org.uk/. Accessed 25 April 2024.

Akazaki, Misa. 2010. Negotiating different assumptions: The experience of mature Japanese students in British Universities. *Journal of Studies in International Education* 14 (4): 355–370. https://doi.org/10.1177/1028315309334642.

Akilli, Kubra, and Emre Ipekci Cetin. 2020. Selection of scholarship students in higher education with VIKOR Method. *International Journal of Assessment Tools in Education* 7 (3): 379–391. https://eric.ed.gov/?id=EJ1272874.

Alexander, Olwyn, Sue Argent, and Jenifer Spence. 2019. *EAP essentials: A teacher's guide to principles and practice*, 2nd ed. Reading: Garnet.

Alkhateeb, Abdulelah. 2018. Dynamic transfer and relations between first language (L1) proficiency and second language (L2) writing skills performance. *Arab World English Journal* 9 (4): 324–336. https://files.eric.ed.gov/fulltext/EJ1311676.pdf.

Anderson, Tim. 2020. International and refugee university students in Canada: Trends, barriers, and the future. *Comparative and International Education/Éducation comparée et internationale* 48 (2). https://doi.org/10.5206/cie-eci.v48i2.10787.

Arias, J.J., John Swinton, and Kay Anderson. 2018. Online vs. face-to-face: A comparison of student outcomes with random assignment. *The E-Journal of Business Education and Scholarship of Teaching* 12 (2): 1–23. https://www.proquest.com/docview/2125614115?accountid=14664&pq-origsite=primo&sourcetype=Scholarly%20Journals.

Aspect International Language Academies. 2024. University pathways. Kaplan International. https://www.kaplaninternational.com/higher-education/pathways. Accessed 10 July 2024.

Ataç, Bengü Aksu, Hatice Özgan Sucu, Baris Eriçok, and Merve Bulut. 2018. The identification of difference between achievement levels of optional and compulsory English preparatory class students. *The Journal of Language and Linguistic Studies* 14 (3): 269–280. https://eric.ed.gov/?id=EJ1193271.

Bai, Li, and Ying Xian Wang. 2022. Combating language and academic culture shocks—International students' agency in mobilizing their cultural capital. *Journal of Diversity in Higher Education* 17 (2): 215–228. https://doi.org/10.1037/dhe0000409.

Bamford, Jan Katherine, Gary Pheiffer, Inge Weber-Newth, and Tim Marr. 2006. International postgraduate students in London: Some features of their expectations and experience. *The Cyprus Journal of Sciences* 4: 25–38. https://ac.ac.cy/wp-content/uploads/2022/12/Cyprus-Journal-of-Sciences-Vol.-4.pdf.

Beaven, Ananad Helen Spencer-Oatey. 2016. Cultural adaptation in different facets of life and the impact of language: A case study of personal adjustment patterns during study abroad. *Language and Intercultural Communication* 16 (3): 349–367. https://doi.org/10.1080/14708477.2016.1168048.

Bennion, Alice, Anna Scesa, and Ruth Williams. 2011. The benefits of part-time undergraduate study and UK higher education policy: A literature review. *Higher Education Quarterly* 65 (2): 145–163. https://doi.org/10.1111/j.1468-2273.2010.00482.x.

Binali, Theerapong, Chin-Chung Tsai, and Hsin-Yi Chang. 2021. University students' profiles of online learning and their relation to online metacognitive regulation and internet-specific epistemic justification. *Computers and Education* 175: 104315. https://doi.org/10.1016/j.compedu.2021.104315.

Bridges, Paul, Angela Cooper, Peter Evanson, Chris Haines, Don Jenkins, David Scurry, Harvey Woolf, and Mantz Yorke. 2002. Coursework marks high, examination marks low: Discuss. *Assessment and Evaluation in Higher Education* 27 (1): 35–48. https://doi.org/10.1080/02602930120105045.

British Council. n.d. Teaching English for Academic Purposes (EAP). https://www.teachingenglish.org.uk/professional-development/teachers/knowing-subject/articles/teaching-english-academic-purposes-eap. Accessed 8 December 2024.

Brooks, Rachel. 2015. International students with dependent children: The reproduction of gender norms. *British Journal of Sociology of Education* 36 (2): 195–214. http://www.jstor.org/stable/43818780.

Butcher, John, and George Curry. 2022. Digital poverty as a barrier to access. *Widening Participation and Lifelong Learning* 24 (2): 180–194. https://doi.org/10.5456/WPLL.24.2.180.

Cambridge Dictionary. 2024. Red tape. https://dictionary.cambridge.org/dictionary/english/red-tape. Accessed: 1 February 2024.

Campbell, Anne C., and Emelye Neff. 2020. A systematic review of international higher education scholarships for students from the global south.

Review of Educational Research 90 (6): 824–861. https://doi.org/10.3102/0034654320947783.

Cebolla-Boado, Héctor, Yang Hu, and Yasemin Nuhoḡlu Soysal. 2018. Why study abroad? Sorting of Chinese students across British universities. *British Journal of Sociology of Education* 39 (3): 365–380. https://www.jstor.org/stable/26783510.

Chacko, Elizabeth. 2020. Emerging precarity among international students in Singapore: Experiences, understandings and responses. *Journal of Ethnic and Migration Studies* 47 (2): 4741–4757. https://doi.org/10.1080/1369183X.2020.1732618.

Chapple, Julian. 2015. Teaching in English is not necessarily the teaching of English. *International Education Studies* 8 (3): 1–13. https://files.eric.ed.gov/fulltext/EJ1060798.pdf.

Charles, Maggie, and Diane Pecorari. 2015. *Introducing English for academic purposes*. London: Routledge. https://doi.org/10.4324/9781315682129.

Christie, Hazel, Paul Barron, and Norma D'Annunzio-Green. 2013. Direct entrants in transition: Becoming independent learners. *Studies in Higher Education* 38 (4): 623–637. https://doi.org/10.1080/03075079.2011.588326.

Clark, Colin, Rita Kusevskis-Hayes, and Matthew Wilkinson. 2018. Enhancing student disclosure: Australia's invisible equity students and reasons for nondisclosure in Australia's tertiary sector. *JANZSSA—Journal of the Australian and New Zealand Student Services Association* 26 (1). https://doi.org/10.30688/janzssa.2018.05.

Dall'Alba, Gloria, and Ravinder Sidhu. 2013. Australian undergraduate students on the move: Experiencing outbound mobility. *Studies in Higher Education* 40 (4): 721–744. https://doi.org/10.1080/03075079.2013.842212.

Digital Poverty Alliance. 2024. Executive summary. https://digitalpovertyalliance.org/uk-digital-poverty-evidence-review-2022/executive-summary/#:~:text=Digital%20poverty%20is%20the%20inability%20to%20interact%20with,existing%20inequalities%20in%20society%20or%20introduce%20new%20inequalities. Accessed 13 October 2024.

Doyle, Stephanie, Judith Loveridge, and Niusila Faamanatu-Eteuati. 2016. Counting family: Making the family of international students visible in higher education policy and practice. *Higher Education Policy* 29: 184–198. https://doi.org/10.1057/hep.2015.20.

Drennan, Laura. 2022. Transitioning from undergraduate to postgraduate studies: A multistage evaluation of a discipline-specific writing intervention.

Journal for Language Teaching = Ijenali Yekufundzisa Lulwimi = Tydskrif vir Taalonderrig 56 (2): 1–24. https://doi.org/10.56285/jltVol56iss2a5293.

Dryden, Stephanie, Ana Tankosić, and Sender Dovchin. 2021. Foreign language anxiety and translanguaging as an emotional safe space: Migrant English as a foreign language learners in Australia. *System* 101: 102593. https://doi.org/10.1016/j.system.2021.102593.

Edwards, Miriam. 2022. Inclusive learning and teaching for Australian online university students with disability: A literature review. *International Journal of Inclusive Education* 26 (5): 510–525. https://doi.org/10.1080/13603116.2019.1698066.

Espinoza, Oscar, Luis Eduardo González, Noel McGinn, Dante Castillo, and Luis Sandoval. 2019. Factors that affect post-graduation satisfaction of Chilean university students. *Studies in Higher Education* 44 (6): 1023–1038. https://doi.org/10.1080/03075079.2017.1407306.

Evans, Stephen, and Christopher Green. 2007. Why EAP is necessary: A survey of Hong Kong tertiary students. *Journal of English for Academic Purposes* 6 (1): 3–17. https://doi.org/10.1016/j.jeap.2006.11.005.

Evans, Carl, Tien Nguyen, Mark Richardson, and Scott I. Ian. 2018. Managing the transition from undergraduate to taught postgraduate study: Perceptions of international students studying in the UK. *Research in Post-Compulsory Education* 23 (2): 249–265. https://doi.org/10.1080/13596748.2018.1444386.

Fenton-Smith, Ben, Pamela Humphreys, Ian Walkinshaw, Rowan Michael, and Ana Lobo. 2015. Implementing a university-wide credit-bearing English language enhancement programme: Issues emerging from practice. *Studies in Higher Education* 42 (3): 463–479. https://doi.org/10.1080/03075079.2015.1052736.

Fenton-Smith, Ben, Pamela Humphreys, and Ian Walkinshaw. 2018. On evaluating the effectiveness of university-wide credit-bearing English language enhancement courses. *Journal of English for Academic Purposes* 31: 72–83. https://doi.org/10.1016/j.jeap.2017.12.001.

Feubli, Patricia, Douglas MacKevett, and Jürg Schwarz. 2023. Hybrid teaching and learning: A conjoint analysis of student preferences in online and onsite scenarios. *Journal of Computer Assisted Learning* 40 (2): 761–774. https://doi.org/10.1111/jcal.12913.

Fittante, Daniel. 2023. Beyond brokering for recruitment: Education agents in Armenia. *Population Space and Place* 29 (1). https://doi.org/10.1002/psp.2622.

Francis, Emma R., and Hannah D. Franklin. 2023. UK PhD students' call to action amid the cost-of-living crisis. *Nature Human Behaviour* 7: 1029–1030. https://doi.org/10.1038/s41562-023-01614-9.

Gaffas, Zainab M. 2019. Students' perceptions of the impact of EGP and ESP courses on their English language development: Voices from Saudi Arabia. *Journal of English for Academic Purposes* 42: 100797. https://doi.org/10.1016/j.jeap.2019.100797.

Gašević, Dragan, Yi-Shan Tsai, and Hendrik Drachsler. 2022. Learning analytics in higher education—Stakeholders, strategy and scale. *The Internet and Higher Education* 52: 100833. https://doi.org/10.1016/j.iheduc.2021.100833.

Gbadegesin, Job Taiwo, Markson Opeyemi Komolafe, Taiwo Frances Gbadegesin, and Kehinde O. Omotoso. 2021. Off-campus student housing satisfaction indicators and the drivers: From student perspectives to policy re-awakening in governance. *Journal of Human Behavior in the Social Environment* 31 (7): 889–915. https://doi.org/10.1080/10911359.2020.1825247.

Gibney, Amanda, Niamh Moore, Feargal Murphy, and Sara O'Sullivan. 2011. The first semester of university life; 'will I be able to manage it at all?' *Higher Education* 62: 351–366. https://doi.org/10.1007/s10734-010-9392-9.

Global Migration Data Portal. 2024. International students. https://www.migrationdataportal.org/themes/international-students. Accessed 28 May 2024.

Guo, Philip J., Juho Kim, and Rob Rubin. 2014. How video production affects student engagement: An empirical study of MOOC videos. In Proceedings of the first ACM conference on Learning @ scale conference (L@S '14), 41–50. New York, NY: Association for Computing Machinery. https://doi.org/10.1145/2556325.2566239.

Hallam, Isabel. 2023. College higher education commuter students' experiences of belonging, mattering and persisting with their studies. *Research in Post-Compulsory Education* 28 (3): 373–389. https://doi.org/10.1080/13596748.2023.2221116.

Harrison, Daniel, Scarlett Rowland, Gavin Wood, Lynsey Bakewell, Iaonnis Petridis, Kiel Long, Konstantina Vasileiou, Julie Barnett, Manuela Barreto, Michael Wilson, Shaun Lawson, and John Vines. 2023. Designing technology-mediated peer support for postgraduate research students at risk of loneliness and isolation. *ACM Transactions on Computer-Human Interaction* 30 (1): 1–40. https://doi.org/10.1145/3534961.

Hassan, Shahid, Wai Chuen Poon, and Ibiwani Alisa. 2023. Australian housing market: A descriptive study on key issues around housing affordability relevance to international university students in Melbourne, Australia. *E3S Web of Conferences* 389: 9029. https://doi.org/10.1051/e3sconf/202338909029.

Hu, Ruolin, and Danijela Trenkic. 2019. The effects of coaching and repeated test-taking on Chinese candidates' IELTS scores, their English proficiency, and subsequent academic achievement. *International Journal of Bilingual Education and Bilingualism* 24 (10): 1486–1501. https://doi.org/10.1080/13670050.2019.1691498.

Hu, Ke, Junfeng Daio, and Xiaojing Li. 2022. International students' university choice to study abroad in higher education and influencing factors analysis. *Frontiers in Psychology* 13: 1036569. https://doi.org/10.3389/fpsyg.2022.1036569.

Huang, Hsiaowen, Hongyu Shih, Sheela Thiruvadi, and Yiru Song. 2011. A preliminary research on the lifestyle of international students. *US-China Education Review* A (3): 401–411. https://eric.ed.gov/?id=ED524801.

Husain, Sakinah, Hasmah Safiei, Anisah Ghazali, Nur Nazihah Mohd Nazir, Nor Izzati Nor Redzuan, and Fadhilah Abdul Ghani. 2018. Factors affecting students' preferences towards private university college in Malaysia. *Global Business and Management Research* 10 (3): 535–546. https://www.proquest.com/docview/2159617055/fulltextPDF/7D1818AA0104E0CPQ/1?accountid=14664&sourcetype=Scholarly%20Journals.

Hutchinson, Francis E., Shaun Lin, and Tim Bunnell. 2023. The Johor-Singapore causeway: Celebrating and conceptualising its centenary. *Journal of Southeast Asian Studies* 54 (3): 355–366. https://doi.org/10.1017/S0022463423000486.

Jæger, Kirsten, and Malene Gram. 2019. Enduring not enjoying? Emotional responses to studying abroad among Danish and Chinese students. *Intercultural Education* 31 (1): 1–15. https://doi.org/10.1080/14675986.2019.1673651.

Johnson, Patricia. 1988. English language proficiency and academic performance of undergraduate international students. *TESOL Quarterly* 22 (1): 164–168. https://doi.org/10.2307/3587070.

Jordan, R. R. 1997. *English for academic purposes. A guide and resource book for teachers.* Cambridge: Cambridge University Press.

Juma, Fatema Zehra, T. Tamkin Abas, and Shiria Banu. 2016. The transition from high school to university: A medical student's perspective. *Advances in Medical Education and Practice* 7: 517–518. https://doi.org/10.2147/AMEP.S114753.

Kang, Haijun, and Bo Chang. 2016. Examining culture's impact on the learning behaviors of international students from Confucius culture studying in Western online learning context. *Journal of International Students* 6 (3): 779–797. https://files.eric.ed.gov/fulltext/EJ1100335.pdf.

Kazazoglu, Semin. 2020. The impact of L1 interference on foreign language writing: A contrastive error analysis. *The Journal of Language and Linguistic Studies* 16 (3): 1177–1188. https://doi.org/10.17263/jlls.803621.

Kettle, Margaret. 2017. *International student engagement in higher education: Transforming practices, pedagogies and participation.* Bristol: Multilingual Matters.

Kim, Jeongyeon, Bradley Tatar, and Jinsook Choi. 2014. Emerging culture of English-medium instruction in Korea: Experiences of Korean and international students. *Language and Intercultural Communication* 14 (4): 441–459. https://doi.org/10.1080/14708477.2014.946038.

Kiziltas, Yusuf. 2022. Bilingual students, language conflict, language-culture shock: Situations faced by teachers assigned to eastern regions of Turkey. *Kuramsal eğitimbilim dergisi* 15 (1): 191–215. https://eric.ed.gov/?id=EJ1330412.

Kobayashi, Yoko. 2011. Expanding-circle students learning 'standard English' in the outer-circle Asia. *Journal of Multilingual and Multicultural Development* 32 (3): 235–248. https://doi.org/10.1080/01434632.2010.536239.

Latief, Rashid, and Lefen Lin. 2018. Analysis of Chinese government scholarship for international students using analytical hierarchy process (AHP). *Sustainability* 10 (7): 2112. https://doi.org/10.3390/su10072112.

Law, Jonathan. 2009. *A dictionary of business and management*, 5th ed. Edited by Jonathan Law. Oxford: Oxford University Press.

Le, Shiguan, Wang Xi, Wei Li, Jian Xiao, and Zhinong Wang. 2017. Entry-level forward surgical team training in 5th grade students of Second Military Medical University of the Chinese People's Liberation Army. *World Journal of Surgery* 41 (10): 2435–2443. https://link.springer.com/content/pdf/10.1007/s00268-017-4035-2.pdf.

Lenette, Caroline. 2016. University students from refugee backgrounds: Why should we care? *Higher Education Research and Development* 35 (6): 1311–1315. https://doi.org/10.1080/07294360.2016.1190524.

Lewine, Rich, Ashlee Warnecke, and Alison Sommers. 2022. College students from poverty: Academic success and authenticity. *Journal of Poverty* 26 (1): 23–31. https://doi.org/10.1080/10875549.2020.1869666.

Lewis, Gwyn, Bryn Jones, and Colin Baker. 2012. Translanguaging: Origins and development from school to street and beyond. *Educational Research and Evaluation* 18 (7): 641–654. https://doi.org/10.1080/13803611.2012.718488.

Li, Yuehua, and Marion Heron. 2021. English for general academic purposes or English for specific purposes? Language learning needs of medical students at a Chinese university. *Theory and Practice in Language Studies* 11 (6): 621–631. https://doi.org/10.17507/tpls.1106.05.

Li, Chengchen, Jean-Marc Dewaele, and Yanhong Hu. 2021. Foreign language learning boredom: Conceptualization and measurement. *Applied Linguistics Review* 14 (2): 223–249. https://doi.org/10.1515/applirev-2020-0124.

Lipnevich, Anastasiya A., Thomas Guskey, Dana M. Murano, and Jeffrey K. Smith. 2020. What do grades mean? Variation in grading criteria in American college and university courses. *Assessment in Education: Principles, Policy and Practice* 27 (5): 480–500. https://doi.org/10.1080/0969594X.2020.1799190.

Liu, Jin-Yu, Yu-Jung Chang, Fang-Ying Yang, and Yu-Chih Sun. 2011. Is what I need what I want? Reconceptualising college students' needs in English courses for general and specific/academic purposes. *Journal of English for Academic Purposes* 10 (4): 271–280. https://doi.org/10.1016/j.jeap.2011.09.002.

Luo, Jiali, and David Jamieson-Drake. 2015. Predictors of study abroad intent, participation, and college outcomes. *Research in Higher Education* 56: 29–56. https://doi.org/10.1007/s11162-014-9338-7.

MacIntyre, Peter D., Tammy Gregersen, and Sarah Mercer. 2019. Setting an agenda for positive psychology in SLA: Theory, practice, and research. *The Modern Language Journal* 103 (1): 262–274. http://www.jstor.org/stable/45171996.

Marquis, Gerald P., and Soumen Ghosh. 2017. Student preferences for a hybrid course. *Journal of Education for Business* 92 (3): 105–113. https://doi.org/10.1080/08832323.2017.1289886.

Marr, Tim. 2005. Language and the capital: A case study of English 'language shock' among Chinese students in London. *Language Awareness* 14 (4): 239–253. https://doi.org/10.1080/09658410508668839.

Masoudi, Hatim. 2025. Motivational benefits of translanguaging for EFL learners. *Theory and Practice in Language Studies* 15 (5): 1697–1709. https://doi.org/10.17507/tpls.1505.35.

McKenna, Deirdre, and Aleks Palanac. 2025. RefugEAP case study: Developing and critically evaluating a free, online trauma-informed English for Academic Purposes (EAP) programme for refugee-background students.

Journal of Interactive Media in Education 1: 6. https://doi.org/10.5334/jime.894.

Meyer, Linda, and Birgit Schreiber. 2024. South African private universities: The unique challenges of private university first-generation students—The unique opportunity for private higher education institutions. *Journal of Student Affairs in Africa* 12 (1): 68–95. https://doi.org/10.24085/jsaa.v12i1.5245.

Miller, Lisa R., Kimberly K. Klassen, and Jacques W. Hardy. 2021. Curriculum design from theory to practice: Preparing Japanese students to study abroad using content-based language teaching. *The Curriculum Journal* 32 (2): 215–246. https://doi.org/10.1002/curj.68.

Minami, Masago, Ryoko Niikura, Masami Kashimura, and Yoshiro Okubo. 2021. Factors influencing the mental health of international students, as observed in a longitudinal study on former Japanese government scholarship students. *Journal of Nippon Medical School* 88 (5): 475–484. https://www.jstage.jst.go.jp/article/jnms/88/5/88_JNMS.2021_88-606/_pdf/-char/en.

Monika, M., and Anitha Devi V. 2022. A systematic review on the effectiveness of metacognitive strategies and multimodal tools in blended learning English language classroom. *Theory and Practice in Language Studies* 12 (11): 2239–2252. https://doi.org/10.17507/tpls.1211.03.

Mousavian Rad, S.E., A. Roohani, and A. Mirzaei. 2022. Developing and validating precursors of students' boredom in EFL classes: An exploratory sequential mixed-methods study. *Journal of Multilingual and Multicultural Development*: 1–8. https://doi.org/10.1080/01434632.2022.2082448.

Navarro-Cruz, Giselle Emilia, Brianne A. Dávila, A. Ana Amaya, and Ishia Orozco-Barajas. 2023. Accommodating life's demands: Childcare choices for student parents in higher education. *Early Childhood Research Quarterly* 62: 217–228. https://doi.org/10.1016/j.ecresq.2022.08.009.

NCUK. 2024. International foundation year https://www.ncuk.ac.uk/ncuk-qualifications/ncuk-international-foundation-year/. Accessed 16 November 2024.

NCUK. n.d. https://www.ncuk.ac.uk/wp-content/uploads/2024/12/International-Foundation-Year-Entry-Requirements-December-2024.pdf. Accessed 25 February 2025.

Newcastle University. 2025. Undergraduate vs. postgraduate: What's the difference? https://belong.ncl.ac.uk/blog/difference-between-undergrad-and-postgrad#what_are_the_differences. Accessed 12 January 2024.

Newton, Janice, and Sue Turale. 2000. Student poverty at the University of Ballarat. *Australian Journal of Social Issues* 35 (3): 251–265. https://doi.org/10.1002/j.1839-4655.2000.tb01309.x.

Nuseir, Mohammed T., and Ghaleb A. El Refae. 2022. Factors influencing the choice of studying at UAE universities: An empirical research on the adoption of educational marketing strategies. *Journal of Marketing for Higher Education* 32 (2): 215–237. https://doi.org/10.1080/08841241.2020.1852467.

Orphan, Cecilia M. 2020. Not all regional public universities strive for prestige: Examining and strengthening mission-centeredness within a vital sector. *New Directions for Higher Education* 190: 9–24. https://doi.org/10.1002/he.20364.

Ortega-Llebaria, Marta, and Laura Colantoni. 2014. L2 English intonation: Relations between form-meaning associations, access to meaning and L1 transfer. *Studies in Second Language Acquisition* 36 (2): 331–353. https://www.jstor.org/stable/26328943.

Pawlak, Mirosław, Mariusz Kruk, Joanna Zawodniak, and S. ławomir Pasikowski. 2020. Investigating factors responsible for boredom in English classes: The case of advanced learners. *System* 91: 102259. https://doi.org/10.1016/j.system.2020.102259.

Pearson, William S. 2020a. Mapping English language proficiency cut-off scores and pre-sessional EAP programmes in UK higher education. *Journal of English for Academic Purposes* 45: 100866. https://doi.org/10.1016/j.jeap.2020.100866.

Pearson, William S. 2020b. The effectiveness of pre-sessional EAP programmes in UK higher education: A review of the evidence. *Review of Education* 8: 420–447. https://doi.org/10.1002/rev3.3191.

Pekrun, Reinhard, Stephanie Lichtenfeld, Herbert W. Marsh, Kou Murayama, and Thomas Goetz. 2017. Achievement emotions and academic performance: Longitudinal models of reciprocal effects. *Child Development* 88 (5): 1653–1670. https://doi.org/10.1111/cdev.12704.

Pimpa, Nattavud. 2005. A family affair: The effect of family on Thai students' choices of international education. *Higher Education* 49 (4): 431–448. https://doi.org/10.1007/s10734-004-2825-6.

Presbitero, Alfred. 2016. Culture shock and reverse culture shock: The moderating role of cultural intelligence in international students' adaptation. *International Journal of Intercultural Relations* 53: 28–38. https://doi.org/10.1016/j.ijintrel.2016.05.004.

Reeves, Stephanie Lauren. 2015. Caught up in red tape: Bureaucratic hassles undermine sense of belonging in college among first generation students. Master of Arts thesis, University of Texas at Austin. https://repositories.lib.utexas.edu/items/078caa4c-9188-4975-b904-9a79d2b7153e.

Richardson, John T. E. 2014. Coursework versus examinations in end-of-module assessment: A literature review. *Assessment and Evaluation in Higher Education* 40 (3): 439–455. https://doi.org/10.1080/02602938.2014.919628.

Ro, Jina. 2019. The meaning of teacher education in an exam-oriented education system: Lessons from novice secondary teachers in Korea. *Asia-Pacific Journal of Teacher Education* 47 (4): 399–413. https://doi.org/10.1080/1359866X.2018.1499013.

Roche, Thomas, and Sara Booth. 2021. A collaborative approach to assuring standards: Using the CEFR to benchmark university pathway programs' English language outcomes. *Language Teaching Research Quarterly* 26: 18–38. https://files.eric.ed.gov/fulltext/EJ1325970.pdf.

Royal College of Music. 2025. Bachelor of music. https://www.rcm.ac.uk/courses/undergraduate/bmus/. Accessed 30 June 2025.

Sanderson Cole, Karen. 2012. Promoting cooperative learning in an expository writing course. *Journal of International Education Research* 8 (2): 113–124. https://doi.org/10.19030/jier.v8i2.6831.

Seyri, Haniye, and Ali Abbas Rezaee. 2024. An autonomy-oriented response to EAP students' learned helplessness in online classes. *Current Psychology* 43: 7887–7898. https://doi.org/10.1007/s12144-023-04981-8.

Sherry, Mark, Peter Thomas, and Wing Hong Chui. 2010. International students: A vulnerable student population. *Higher Education* 60: 33–46. https://doi.org/10.1007/s10734-009-9284-z.

Sloan, Diane, and Elizabeth Porter. 2010. Changing international student and business staff perceptions of in-sessional EAP: Using the CEM model. *Journal of English for Academic Purposes* 9 (3): 198–210. https://doi.org/10.1016/j.jeap.2010.03.001.

Soar, Max, Lucy Stewart, Sylvia Nissen, Sereana Naepi, and Tara McAllister. 2022. Sweat equity: Student scholarships in Aotearoa New Zealand's universities. *New Zealand Journal of Educational Studies* 57 (2): 505–523. https://doi.org/10.1007/s40841-022-00244-5.

Sümer, Seda, Senel Poyrazli, and Kamini Grahame. 2008. Predictors of depression and anxiety among international students. *Journal of Counselling and Development* 86 (4): 429–437. https://doi.org/10.1002/j.1556-6678.2008.tb00531.x.

Tastanbek, Serikbolsyn. 2024. Translanguaging pedagogy in EAP writing: A multilingual Qazaq instructor's perspective. *Journal of English for Academic Purposes* 63: 101075. https://doi.org/10.1016/j.jslw.2023.101075.

Tatzl, Dietmar. 2011. English-medium masters' programmes at an Austrian university of applied sciences: Attitudes, experiences and challenges. *Journal of English for Academic Purposes* 10 (4): 252–270. https://doi.org/10.1016/j.jeap.2011.08.003.

Taylor, Barrett J., and Brendan Cantwell. 2019. *Unequal higher education: Wealth, status, and student opportunity.* New Brunswick: Rutgers University Press. https://www.perlego.com/book/1259719.

Tian, Mei, and John Lowe. 2013. The role of feedback in cross-cultural learning: A case study of Chinese taught postgraduate students in a UK university. *Assessment and Evaluation in Higher Education* 38 (5): 580–598. https://doi.org/10.1080/02602938.2012.670196.

Tibbetts, Neil Adam, and Timothy Chapman. 2023. *A guide to In-sessional English for academic purposes.* Abingdon: Routledge. https://www.perlego.com/book/3854237.

UCAS. 2024. The difference between school and university or college. https://www.ucas.com/money-and-student-life/student-life/starting-university-or-college/difference-between-school-and-university-or-college. Accessed 11 May 2024.

University of Hong Kong. 2024. A transformative graduate curriculum. https://tl.hku.hk/flexible-curriculum-structure/. Accessed 8 May 2024.

University of Leeds. 2025. Undergraduate pre-sessional English. https://www.leeds.ac.uk/language-centre-courses/doc/undergraduate-pre-sessional-english. Accessed 3 February 2025.

University of Leicester. n.d. RefugEAP Programme. https://le.ac.uk/cite/sanctuary-seekers-unit/initiatives/refugeap. Accessed 22 September 2024.

University of Nottingham. 2025. Which pre-sessional course is right for you? https://www.nottingham.ac.uk/cele/pre-sessional/which-course.aspx. Accessed 3 March 2025.

Wakeling, Paul, and Katie Jefferies. 2013. The effect of tuition fees on student mobility: The UK and Ireland as a natural experiment. *British Educational Research Journal* 39 (3): 491–513. http://www.jstor.org/stable/24463969.

Wang, Haihua, Lin Xu, and Jiaxin Li. 2023. Connecting foreign language enjoyment and English proficiency levels: The mediating role of L2 motivation. *Frontiers in Psychology* 14. https://doi.org/10.3389/fpsyg.2023.1054657.

Ward, Colleen A., Stephen Bochner, and Adrian Furnham. 2005. *The psychology of culture shock*, New ed. London: Routledge.
White, Alison. 2023. The *Transition In* framework: Supporting the transition of students into postgraduate taught study. *Innovations in Education and Teaching International* 61 (4): 703–715. https://doi.org/10.1080/14703297.2023.2216682.
Wilang, Jeffrey Dawala, and Supasinee Nupong. 2022. Factors affecting EMI attitudes of engineering and nursing students. *Theory and Practice in Language Studies* 12 (3): 437–446. https://doi.org/10.17507/tpls.1203.03.
Wilson, Victoria, Homeira Babaei, Merna Dolmai, and Suhail Sawa. 2022. Insider views on English language pathway programmes to Australian universities. In *Opening up the university: Teaching and learning with refugees*, ed. Céline Cantat, Ian M. Cook, and Prem Kumar Rajaram, 164–177. New York: Berghahn Books.
Yung, Kevin Wai-Ho, and Natalie Fong. 2019. Learning EAP at University: Perceptions of high-achieving first-year ESL undergraduates. *ELT Journal* 73 (3): 306–315. https://doi.org/10.1093/elt/ccz019.
Zasina, Jakub, and El. żbieta Antczak. 2023. The 'gown' unconcerned with the town? Residential satisfaction of university students living in off-campus private accommodation. *Housing Studies* 38 (8): 1536–1559. https://doi.org/10.1080/02673037.2021.1961692.
Zawodniak, Joanna, Maruisz Kruk, and Mirosław Pawlak. 2021. Boredom as an aversive emotion experienced by English majors. *RELC Journal* 54 (1): 22–36. https://doi.org/10.1177/0033688220973732.
Zhang, Bowen. 2021. A comparison between pedagogical approaches in UK and China. *Journal of Comparative and International Higher Education* 13 (5): 232–242. https://eric.ed.gov/?id=EJ1326691.
Ziegler, Johannes C., Conrad Perry, Anna,Ma-Wyatt, Diana Ladner, and Gerd Schulte-Körne. 2003. Developmental dyslexia in different languages: Language-specific or universal? *Journal of Experimental Child Psychology* 86: 169–193. https://doi.org/10.1016/s0022-0965(03)00139-5.
Zohoorian, Zahra. 2015. Motivation level: A study on the effect of an authentic context. *Procedia—Social and Behavioral Sciences* 192: 15–25. https://doi.org/10.1016/j.sbspro.2015.06.003.

5

People, Place, Compassion, Power

5.1 Introducing PPCP

In the preceding chapters I set the scene for a humanistic approach to EAP pedagogy through reviewing humanism in education, the contexts in which EAP takes place, the EAP student profile why a different approach to teaching learners undertaking EAP is necessary. It is in this chapter that I showcase the purpose of this publication which is the presentation of the PPCP theory.

PPCP is a theory for fostering the conditions for learning. It was created from humanistic principles and is noteworthy in that it combines elements found through multiple PTAs. It can allow for the opportunity for each of the purposes of EAP outlined in Sect. 1.3 . These purposes are:

A. Bridging the perceived language gap of what is considered a language deficit between completed studies and future studies in the English language
B. Raising consciousness and fostering the designated skills deemed necessary for academic study
C. Raising awareness of community skills

L. Dyer, *A Humanistic Approach to English for Academic Purposes Pedagogy*, https://doi.org/10.1007/978-3-032-00186-3_5

This is because PPCP is a theory for the practitioner to generate conditions which gives learners the opportunity to demonstrate and develop their learning potential. It is a theory that can primarily be used for the purpose of designing and planning pedagogical activities. In general, it can be said that the designing of pedagogical activities is a lengthier detailed process in comparison to the planning and involves some form of the creation of new teaching and learning activities from scratch or from a foundational idea. In contrast planning suggests that teaching materials are already in place and are there to be adapted by the teacher to suit the needs of their learners. In both cases, adaptations may be made during the teaching process as it becomes apparent that the activities may need adjustments during the lessons to suit the needs of the learners or other extenuating circumstances such as interruptions to lessons or spending more or less time on pedagogical activities than anticipated. Teachers may also find themselves designing and planning during lessons and I have found myself in situations where an idea suddenly comes to my head that I immediately implement to suit the needs of the learners and the lesson. After teaching a session, teachers may also reflect on its successes and areas for improvement which may generate potential for the use of PPCP in the re-teaching of materials. For these reasons, it can be seen that PPCP can be applied at multiple stages in the teaching and learning cycle and should not be restricted purely to designing and planning (see Sect. 1.6). However it is for the designing and planning stage that PPCP was conceived and so may prove to be the most conducive. It is for the practitioner to determine the first three elements of the theory—people, place and compassion. The successful amalgamation of these three components can lead to the fourth student driven element—power.

This chapter has been divided into four sections: firstly an outline of the situation which led to the creation of PPCP. Second, a visualisation of PPCP is presented. Next, an explanation of applying PPCP is provided. Finally, and forming the majority of this chapter, an explanation of the theory. Applications of the theory are presented in Chapter 6 with Chapter 7 providing a critique.

5.2 The Creation of PPCP

Like many educators the COVID-19 pandemic had a profound impact on my teaching, moving from a fifteen hour to a six hour a week teaching schedule then adapting the remaining curriculum for asynchronous study. After some initial confidence issues, I soon found myself able to adapt the 'new normal' of teaching and achieved successful outcomes with my teaching despite the trying situation. One aspect of teaching I have always focused on providing a positive learning space with as much student to student spoken communication as possible. The switch to online teaching meant a change to those communicative opportunities but I was determined to make the best of the situation. Fortunately I initially experienced positive engagement from students who on the whole demonstrated high levels of self-regulated learning and as a result generally gained high academic achievement, including in spoken communication (Dörrenbächer and Perels 2016). However, a later cohort of students proved much more challenging. In contrast to the synchronous teaching experiences with my previous online groups, not one of these students had their camera switched on or contributed to the lessons either verbally, through chat or even in breakout rooms and would only speak if I nominated them. Their written work displayed limited critical thinking and I feared this would have a significant impact on their progression without improvement. In my head I began to run through what I might not be doing with this group that I had successfully with others but soon came to realise that there was no difference and that it was down to the individual learner how they responded to this new style of learning. I realised that the students were likely going one or more of a range of emotions that was affecting their learning experience. These emotions likely included:

- Negative feelings over technical resources (Biwer et al. 2021), either in the form of learning the digitality, difficulties with its use such as internet connection or simply adapting to online learning
- Anger or frustration over not being able to travel abroad to study in a face-to-face context

- Feelings of isolation due a lack of sense of belonging (Morán-Soto et al. 2022)
- Insecurity over whether they are able to cope with the new style of learning (Breiby et al. 2023) and/or the EAP course

I tried a range of techniques from my repertoire to encourage more communication from this group of students but none of them worked. To hear colleagues teaching on the same module talk about how engaged their groups were proved disheartening to me as a teacher. As I said previously, I view spoken communication in the classroom as one of my strengths, but this time I had failed in achieving almost any form of communication in the synchronous learning sessions. Although my group of students had been on the course for around six weeks, they had not demonstrated or attempted to demonstrate the speaking competencies that all of other groups I had taught over many years would have shown by that point. A short time later I then saw on the timetable that one of the module's formative tasks was for students to asynchronously create and upload a pre-recorded presentation on their research for their written assessment with peer feedback to be given synchronously. I knew immediately that this task would not work for my group and that I had to do something different to get them to successfully complete this peer feedback. At this stage I went through a pedagogical panic (Dyer 2021) and created an approach which I have subsequently called paired peer feedback and can be found in Sect. 6.8 of this publication. Although the students had previously worked in groups of three to four in breakout rooms, they had not worked together in a pair so I took this approach to groupings. The resulting student actions were in complete contrast to their previous work. The activity had a profound impact on the students and I noticed immediate engagement in the task in terms of communication and success through the form of critical thinking. This was how I measured initial success with the activity. Subsequent lessons saw students volunteering answers, asking questions verbally and in the chat and, perhaps less importantly, some students switched their cameras on. It was as though the paired peer feedback activity had unlocked something within and now the students felt able to demonstrate what they were capable of. This was a further demonstration of success with the activity. I am happy to report that despite my earlier concerns about this group of students, each of them passed and were able to progress to their postgraduate studies.

Following this success with paired peer feedback I decided to take some time to reflect on exactly what it was that had made the activity so successful and transformed the engagement and learning outputs of the students. After deliberating I realised that it was the combination of three specific aspects in which considered humanistic learning practices that led to the successful outcomes. The three aspects were:

- Choosing how students worked on this activity, which in this case was in a pair
- Deciding that to complete this activity the pairs would each be in their own breakout room
- Allowing the feedback generated to be semi-autonomous

The resulting student action was one of power through the engagement in the task and quality of their feedback outputs. It was here I determined that by creating the right conditions for people, place and factoring in compassion the student will have power, or success, in their learning. Thus people, place, compassion, power or PPCP was born.

5.3 Visualising PPCP

Before explaining PPCP in words, I have chosen to create a visual that illustrates how the four components work together. Figure 5.1 has been developed as a means to visualise PPCP. The three components fostered by the teacher—people, place and compassion—are linked together by interlocking circles to show the necessity for each to be in place. If these three components are successfully achieved, then the possibility for power from the student is there, with power illustrated by the arrows surrounding the interlocking circles. This shows that power is separate from people, place and compassion and occurs when conditions are in place for the student to activate flow.

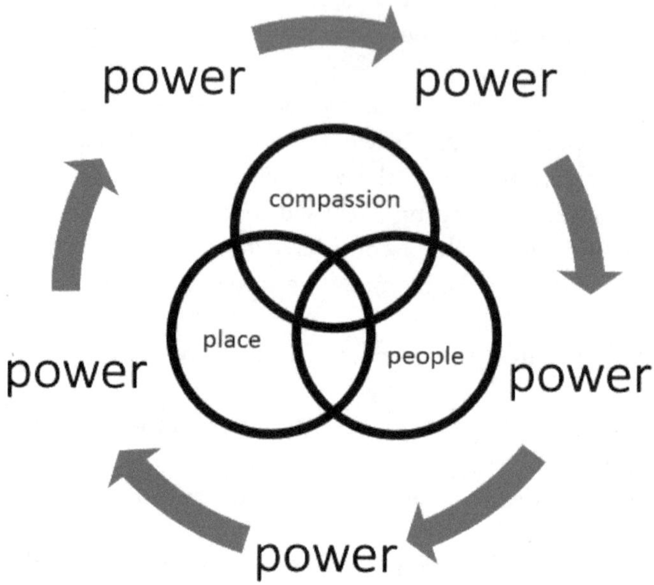

Fig. 5.1 Matrix of elements demonstrating PPCP

5.4 Using PPCP

PPCP is a humanistic theory which relates to the individual learner's emotions in the learning process, and the importance of emotions has already been outlined in Chapter 2. PPCP should be considered by the practitioner placing themselves in the shoes of the learner and thus considering any potential barriers to learning (see Sect. 4.5). This could be questioned through the following:

- Are there any aspects of the pedagogical activity that could act as a barrier to learning and/or students producing output that demonstrates their current or potential abilities?

If you feel the answer is 'no' then PPCP need not be considered. If the answer is 'yes' then further analysis can be applied to each of the first three components of PPCP—people, place and compassion. This analysis may result in practitioners identifying issues with just one of the components or perhaps even all three. In this case the practitioner should make changes to the pedagogical activity to allow for a more conducive and positive learning experience. Table 5.1 outlines some suggested points to consider in the designing and planning process. These suggested points are explored in more detail in Sect. 5.5 of this chapter.

Although there are four clear elements there is potential for overlapping. For example, determining the lighting in a classroom could be considered relevant to both place as it refers to the physical learning environment and compassion as it considers how to make students more comfortable. Another example is deciding the allocation of students for collaborative activities. This refers to people but selecting those allocations based on student interpersonal relationships could be considered as compassion. For the purposes of this chapter, any factors that could be considered as 'compassion', such as classroom lighting and interpersonal

Table 5.1 Questions for consideration in applying PPCP

Component	Suggested points to consider
People	This asks practitioners to consider who is taking part in the learning process. What is the role of the teacher? If the activity includes group work, how many students are needed?
Place	Practitioners should contemplate where a learning activity takes place. Is there a place for learners to prepare? Where does learning take place? A place to record their work? A place for learners to improve or learn from feedback? Is the learning taking place in a classroom, online or in a hybrid situation?
Compassion	This component covers a range of factors such as interpersonal relationships in the classroom. Are time restrictions in an activity necessary? How can the learning environment be made more conducive? Is there a possibility for students to be 'anonymous' in their learning?
Power	By considering the preceding three elements, there is greater opportunity for the individual learner. Students have the opportunity to learn from each other, negotiate, work collaboratively, notice and above all become more confident

relationships, are discussed in the compassion section but the reader is free to consider if they may also be relevant to other components.

5.5 Presenting the Four Components of PPCP

This section outlines each of PPCP's components individually. Although the components are separated for presentation, as already stated there is potential for overlapping such as considering which students might work best together in a group (covering both the people and compassion components) and making the learning environment as comfortable as conducive as possible (covering both the place and compassion components). The components are presented in the order of the letters of the acronym—people, place, compassion, power.

5.5.1 People

As stated in Sect. 4.1, it would be a useless exercise to create a pedagogical theory without considering the people who will be on the receiving end of the pedagogy. Additionally, being a humanistic theory, PPCP considers the person to be its primary focus and this is why the first 'P' in its acronym is people. For the purposes of PPCP, the people involved in the pedagogical activities are the teacher and the learner. There is an emerging additional 'person' to consider in the learning process—the non-human—but this is not discussed as the focus of PPCP theory is on the human. 'People' considers how we as practitioners can allow the learner to thrive whilst considering their individual needs, identities and worries. Appreciating the learner as individuals increases the chances of positive engagement, achievement and well-being (Oleson 2023). Likewise, appreciating the dynamics of a learner group can lead to positive learning experiences for the individuals within (Dörnyei and Murphey 2003). This section examines two people: the learner, working both as an individual and in collaboration with others, and the teacher.

5.5.1.1 The Learner

The learner is the focus of PPCP and is the reason for its creation. Without considering the learner, their experiences and emotions we limit their potential achievements in the learning process. For the purposes of PPCP, learners can be split into three categories: the individual, a pair of learners and a group of three or more learners working together. Humanistic education promotes collaboration yet there are instances when individual learning may be the best or only option for an activity. Therefore PPCP asks the practitioner to consider each of the three categories stated above in their pedagogies.

As previously stated, the vast majority of EAP takes place in HE settings (Riazi et al. 2020), meaning that learners should have some awareness of the requirements of independent study, autonomy and self-responsibility for learning yet this can still take place in collaboration with other learners. In this regard, the role of the learner is one in which they take more control over their learning and that teachers should allow opportunities for this to happen. By applying PPCP to activity design, a teacher could consider the following suggested questions about learners:

- Is the best learning experience for students in this context to work independently or in collaboration with others?
- If it is best to work in collaboration, at what stage in the activity should this take place?
- If learners are working in collaboration, how many peers should they work with?
- Can learners be provided with opportunities to learn from each other, either by working independently or in collaboration?
- How much support might learners need from the teacher in order to complete the tasks?
- Can learners achieve desired outcomes with minimal or without support from teachers?

5.5.1.2 Learning as an Individual

Learning as an individual allows for a demonstration of what the individual is capable of and the development of voice. It allows for more in-depth concentration without distraction from others. Learning as an individual allows for the learner to become aware of their own self and reflect internally on their successes and challenges. The individual can tailor their learning pathway to suit their own needs and interests. Raising awareness of studies is the component that is most likely to be learnt alone as this is tailored to the individual. Even if two students are or will be undertaking the same academic program, distinctions can still be made based upon the learner's specific interests such as module choice. In terms of both the language and skills needed this can also be achieved to an extent as an individual, with reading and writing generally considered to be acquired independently. Listening too is for the most part considered an independent activity, though a collaborative listening activity is outlined in Sect. 6.7. However, it is with speaking that there are questions over learning as an individual is raised. Is it possible to develop speaking skills without interaction from others?

5.5.1.3 Learning as a Pair

Multiple studies and approaches have discussed the role of interaction in language learning (An and Thomas 2021) such as in the Interaction Hypothesis (Long 1996), SCT and Social Constructivism (Palincsar 1998). Pair work offers more opportunity for learners to contribute to the task (Fernández Dobao 2014) as well for keeping focused on the task. Peer-peer activities have been shown to have a positive impact on the L2 learning process as it provides opportunity for interaction, scaffolding and supporting each other in the production of new language (Fernández Dobao 2014). As mentioned previously, PPCP emerged as a result of disengagement from a group of online learners. In order to for each student to be given the opportunity to participate I placed them in pairs so that there was nowhere to hide but also only one person to work with. In other words, if both students did not participate, the task could not be undertaken. In that instance pairs were highly successful in engaging learners to carry out and complete the task to a high standard. Learning as a pair can also be considered as safe approach to learning as interacting with one other, especially in a language that is not your L1, is less anxiety inducing than speaking with a larger number of people.

5.5.1.4 Learning in Larger Groups

Collaborative discussions are just as important as the work that is produced (Lwin et al. 2012) which supports SCT. Collaborative tasks are widely used in the L2 classroom to foster L2 acquisition (Fernández Dobao 2012). Learning collaboratively has been shown to heighten student engagement in the learning process through shared experiences of flow where the collaborative process facilitates enjoyment and immersion in an activity. This experience is known as interactive flow due to its social interaction construct and can have significant positive benefits for intellectual engagement (Raettig and Weger 2018). Interactive flow can also act as a support network where learners feel comfortable in requesting help from their peers and can show support to others they feel may need it.

Additionally, if learners are to work collaboratively, it is important to consider whether or not to place them with others with similar or different characteristics. These characteristics can include: L1, cultural background, gender and engagement. The learner's skillset can also be used to determine how to group students, such as deciding whether or not to place high ability speakers together or not. However, as no two learners share the same characteristics, it means that they can be both novices and experts within the same task (Donato 1994 cited in Fernández Dobao 2014). Learners sharing similar abilities can support each other to achieve a performance than can take them beyond their current level (Donato 1994 cited in Fernández Dobao 2014). Collaborative work sets the learner on a path to aspire to be their best as they internally compare themselves to their group members. Group work provides context for a larger set of knowledge, linguistic sources and noticing how others carry out tasks (Fernández Dobao 2014).

5.5.1.5 The Teacher

There may be questions raised over the inclusion of the teacher as part of PPCP. Even though PPCP is a humanistic framework, this framework cannot be put into place without the teacher. It is the teacher who potentially determines the theme of a learning experience, thus guiding students down a pathway to achieve a range of outcomes. It is the teacher who has the opportunity to notice the needs of their learners and make adaptations to suit these needs. It is the teacher who monitors to direct and facilitate the learning process. For these reasons, it is important to consider the actions of the teacher and thus they are included in PPCP.

As stated in Sect. 1.9, the term 'teacher' is usually used to refer to an individual who plays a pedagogical role in a school. However, the term can also be expanded to encompass a range of professionals in college and university settings. In college and university settings, teachers are normally required to demonstrate a more rigorous skillset and thus may be referred to as 'lecturer', 'tutor' (Wallace 2015) or 'educator'. No matter what the title, it can be said that a teacher is the individual in the classroom that informs, mediates, facilitates, fosters, motivates, encourages and develops learners to achieve desired outcomes. Learners may take feedback from teachers in the form of an appraisal, guidance or assessment (Wallace 2015). Learners also respond to teachers who, even in student-centred learning approaches, remain the authority in the classroom. For example, if there is a group work task the teacher can promote and facilitate this through their own actions (Clifton 2006) such as participating in a group discussion. The teacher is the conductor to whom learners react, determining topic, task, timing and output in the learning experience. Even in prescribed curricula, teachers are the authority in deciding how to teach an activity, the language they use in instruction, when to move on to the next task and appraising learner output. The following questions could be considered regarding the teacher:

- What is the role of the teacher?
- Are they an informer, leader or something else?
- What input does the teacher provide in the learning process?

In PPCP, the teacher is asked to consider their function in the learning process which may place them in a different position to what learners expect. The design or adaptation of activities to give students more control in their learning may lead the teacher to take a more backseat role in content yet the teacher will still determine classroom orchestration (Dillenbourg 2013) through the management of real time pedagogical and non-pedagogical activities, actions and constructs.

An additional aspect for the teacher to consider is their use of language as this can also play a role in the learning process. Some aspects to consider are:

- How often does the teacher speak?
- What type of language is used? Positive/negative, open/closed
- Is what the teacher says clear?

It is recognised that language of praise and acknowledgement from the teacher has been shown to develop a supportive learning environment (Heron and Webster 2019). Therefore as PPCP is a humanistic theory teacher language should err on the positive side.

Learners are the recipients of pedagogy. It is through learners that teachers can see the results of their teaching. Teachers may act as a barrier to learning through methods of teaching (see Islam and Stapa 2021) but by taking humanistic approaches to practices, teachers can become the facilitator (Cornelius-White 2007).

5.5.2 Place

The second 'P' in the acronym PPCP is place. Whilst consideration to the people involved in a learning activity is essential, serious consideration also needs to be given to the place of learning, highlighted by multiple PTAs in Chapter 2. Understanding the importance of place is important in developing an environment in which the learner can thrive. Not considering place can lead to disruption (Low 2016) that can affect flow in the learning process (Beard 2015), leading to potential negative outcomes. The place of learning should be accessible to all people involved in the learning activity and conducive to providing a quality learning experience. It is a context in which actions as well as activities occur that can impact on learning (Weddell and Malderez 2013). Vygotsky's SCT (see Sect. 2.6.2.10) highlighted the role of interaction in knowledge and skills acquisition, with Long's interaction hypothesis (Long 1981) also supporting its use in language acquisition. However, if a place is not set up for such actions there is less likelihood that these attainments can be achieved. PPCP therefore calls for place to be considered in pedagogical activities.

Place itself can be considered an abstract term when referring to learning. Turnbull (2002) refers to four places, or spaces, in which learning can take place, namely the discursive, cognitive, existential and material (Ellis and Goodyear 2016). For the purpose of PPCP only the material place will be considered in its application, be it in a physical classroom or online learning space.

Questions to consider in terms of place are:

- Where does the learning activity take place?
- Is there a place to record output?
- Is it possible to access this place to refer back to completed work?
- Is there a place where learners can view the work of others?
- Is there a place for interaction, either learner to teacher or learner to learner?

To consider the location of the learning activity first, this can be split into the physical and non-physical environment. In terms of the physical learning environment, the first place to look at is the classroom in the learning institution. Classrooms may vary in size from large lecture theatres to small offices with each having its advantages and drawbacks. Attention must also be drawn to the physical learning environment that is not within the learning institution. Locations include the home, public libraries and outdoor spaces. These may or may not go hand in hand with online or distance learning when it is not viable to physically attend an educational institution, or they may be the learner's choice of place for study whilst attending. In considering any physical place, it is also important to consider the tools that are available to enable learning (Ellis and Goodyear 2016). However, in this instance it is important that the teacher reviews what tools are strictly needed to learn and remove any stresses caused to learners who do not have access to required equipment. If additional equipment is required then training may also be needed and this should be taken into account.

5.5.2.1 Place Details

There are multiple places to consider in a learning activity such as a place to prepare, a learning place, a place to record work and a place to receive feedback. Each of these plays a role in the learning process and can influence student outcomes.

If we consider a place to prepare, this could be in a variety of forms. In flipped learning the place to prepare is outside the learning place. This could be in the learner's home or any other location they choose to work in. However, it also possible for the teacher to designate a place to prepare such as requiring learners to carry out a task that specifically requires their presence in a library prior to attending a lesson. Preparation can of course also take place within the learning place itself, where students may need to undertake a short reading task before they start working on the main pedagogical activity.

A final place to consider is a place to receive feedback. Feedback is used to develop learner confidence and competency in their outputs (Han and Hyland 2019). Feedback could come from teachers, peers or both. By providing a place to receive feedback, learners are able to take the opportunity to review and reflect on their work, which in turn can determine the response taken to the feedback and hence future learning trajectory.

Factors to consider in determining places include:

- Where should these places be?
- How can students access these places?
- Do students need training on how to access these places?

5.5.3 Compassion

The third part of PPCP is compassion. This could be considered to be the most subjective aspect of PPCP and the one over which the practitioner might have the most oversight. Whilst compassion could be seen as 'buzzword' it has the potential to transform learning environments through inclusive and equitable pedagogies that can enable learning to thrive (Waddington and Bonaparte 2025). Compassion can be used to counteract negative emotions which could enable a feeling of powerlessness (Cohen 2001 cited by Zembylas 2017), thus affecting the 'power' aspect of PPCP. Negative emotions can decrease learner engagement and impact on their performance (Qi 2024) as a learner's focus is narrowed (MacIntyre and Gregersen 2012). Therefore, if our aim as practitioners is to help the learner to learn, then we must enable some form of compassion in our practices (Waddington 2016) and encourage the positive emotions to facilitate learning to broaden the learner's perspective (MacIntyre and Gregersen 2012). Compassion can take many forms in pedagogical activities, from content to considering which students work best together. Compassionate pedagogy can be defined as being a learning experience which reduces or removes the barriers of distress and disadvantage in the learning process (Canterbury Christ Church University 2024). In PPCP compassion can be viewed from two aspects:

1. The practitioner's application of compassion into their pedagogical activities. For the purposes of this publication time (see Sect. 5.5.3.1), adjustments to the learning environment (Sect. 5.5.3.2) and anonymisation (Sect. 5.5.3.3) are three factors that can be determined by the educator in their set-up of pedagogical activities. These three factors relate to how the learner perceives their learning experience. There are of course multiple other factors that can be linked to the C of PPCP that are not reviewed here.
2. The second aspect of compassion that can be considered is the student response. As one of the facets of humanism is about respecting the individual, the student's own compassion for other learners is also important. This aspect of compassion is discussed in Sect. 5.5.3.4.

5.5.3.1 Time

The notion of time emerged as a linear concept in Western academies which in turn has led to the underpinning of student development frameworks (Shahjahan 2014). In our teaching practices we are expected to allocate specific timings for each pedagogical activity so as to direct students to undertake all teacher desired tasks in specific timeframe, determining the learning trajectories they take. Yet what if these timings are too long or too short for our students to complete tasks? Learners learn at their own pace, but the use of timings may limit how much a learner can do and thus hinder their cognitive intake. Conversely if timings are too long and a student finishes quicker than expected, the teacher may either need to provide them with another time filling activity whilst others finish or choose to leave the student of their own accord. The use of timings also puts the teacher back in the authoritarian role of driving the learning process rather than taking a step back to put the learner at the centre. As a humanistic theory, PPCP asks the practitioner to consider the use of timings in their teaching practices and whether these are a help or a hindrance to the individual. Some questions to ask are:

- Are timings essential in all pedagogical activities? Perhaps just a few or none at all?
- Without the use of timings, how does the student measure their progress through a task or know when to achieve a certain aspect?
- How does the teacher manage teaching if there are no timings?

One activity that is unlikely to adhere to timings is 'homework', such as work done in preparation for flipped learning (see Sect. 3.4.2.2). Students are able to carry out homework at a time of their choice and for as much time as they choose. Could this notion be brought into the classroom?

5.5.3.2 Adjustments to the Learning Environment

This section explores both the physical and virtual learning environments. A comfortable learning environment can be conducive in helping learners to relax and thus facilitate the learning process (Prabhavathy and Mahalakshmi 2012), thus PPCP supports the adjusting of the learning environment to suit the learner. OECD (2015) too supports the importance of a suitable learning environment in developing learning in both formal and informal learning. A physical learning environment that can be adapted and accommodating for a variety of needs and experiences can help learners feel higher levels of comfort and increase the potential for learning (Peng et al. 2022). A successful physical learning environment is one which allows for both learner collaboration and a personalised learning space (Peng et al. 2022). This could take the form of movable furniture or the ability to allow students to move around the room to find a place suitable for them to undertake their work. Should the infrastructure—learning space, either physical or virtual—not be conducive to learning, this can affect the quality of the learning experience.

It is clear that the physical learning environment can impact on the learning experience and physical space that could be regarded as uncomfortable or unsuitable could have a detrimental impact on the learning experience. The physical environment considers what is appropriate and best for the learning experience (Cleveland and Fisher 2014), with appropriate being the necessary requirements for the physical environment and best determining what enhancements could be made for positive outcomes. This type of environment has also be shown to be preferred by learners (Peng et al. 2022). Factors such as seating layout, furniture, building maintenance and internet accessibility could all have an effect on student learning outcomes (Abbas 2020). However, as EAP practitioners it is likely that we do not have control over many of the aforementioned. Yet there are some elements that we can have some control over and can adjust to improve the learning experience. When considering the physical learning place, the following could be asked:

- Can light, sound and temperature be adjusted to suit the needs and wants of learners?
- Can the classroom layout be modelled so that it fosters learning, collaboration and connectivity between students?
- Is there potential for learners to personalise their temporary learning place in the classroom such as the placing of writing instruments and digital devices?
- Is there room for the teacher to move around the classroom to monitor learning?

All of these can influence the conductivity of the learning environment (Baars et al. 2023; Marmot 2014).

Regarding virtual learning places, these have become increasingly common with the emergence of online learning as well as in face-to-face contexts. In terms of virtual learning places, these can be divided into the formal and informal (Ellis and Goodyear 2016). In a formal virtual learning place, there is a teacher supervisory presence. In the informal place, there is little or no teacher supervision. Virtual learning spaces provide opportunity for collaboration (Li and Mak 2022). For a virtual learning space, attention should be paid to aspects such as ease of use (Feng 2024), inclusivity (Rice and Dunn 2023) and belonging (Phirangee and Hewitt 2024).

5.5.3.3 *Anonymisation*

Anonymisation can be used to create conditions in which a learner's shortcomings, whether self or teacher perceived, can be masked. The use of anonymisation in activities can encourage interest and participation from learners as they can avoid conflict from any potential negative actions (Thanh and Gillies 2010). This is because anonymisation provides learners with a guise (Gabbard 2000) through which they can distance themselves from their outward-facing selves (Grier 2023). This anonymisation opportunity can thus present the learner with a feeling of psychological safety which in turn is a significant factor in the learning process (Wake et al. 2023). A psychologically safe environment is one in which occupiers feel comfortable enough to fully engage in an activity (Edmondson 1999). A psychologically safe environment can provide the learners with a level of challenge, but it should not be too great that the learner feels uncomfortable (Wake et al. 2023). It is one in which a learner can make a mistake and not be identified by their peers. If as practitioners we provide students with opportunities for anonymity in learning activities, we can provide them with psychologically safe learning environments. This which is illustrated by the pair peer feedback activity in Sect. 6.8, which uses semi-anonymisation, as a potential response to the feedback situation faced by Lee and Jo in Sect. 1.1. Once learners are comfortable a greater opportunity for successful learning can take place. PPCP encourages anonymisation when appropriate to allow for learners to produce conflict avoiding work and to save face with their peers. Points to consider regarding anonymisation are:

- Could anonymisation benefit specific pedagogical activities?
- How can anonymisation be integrated into pedagogy?
- Is anonymisation between students, between students and teacher or both?

5.5.3.4 The Learner's Compassion for Others

So far the compassion element of PPCP has focused on what the teacher can do to foster learning for the student. However, this may still be considered to be teacher-centred to an extent as the learners respond to the teacher commands. For compassion to be truly considered as compassionate, it is essential that if a human notices distress in another they should act on reducing it (Gilbert 2016b). Without compassion there is increased potential for negative emotions which in turn can lead to more adverse outcomes (Maxwell 2017) which not only goes against humanistic principles but also fosters conditions for negative learning outputs.

To encourage more compassionate humanistic responses from learners there is also a need for they themselves to show compassion to others. A learner's compassionate actions to peers in pedagogical activities has been shown to have a positive psychological impact, in terms of pedagogical task achievement (Maratos et al. 2019; Gilbert 2016a) and a more inclusive learning environment (Waddington and Bonaparte 2025). Traditional models of education emphasis academic achievement and competitiveness without taking into account how a student may achieve this. Group work in particular may invoke challenges for participants through psychosocial stressors (Gilbert 2016b). Should a learner be made aware of, be required to carry out or even be assessed on (Gilbert 2016a) their compassionate actions in pedagogical activities, they are more likely demonstrate compassionate actions and enable subsequent positive experiences.

Factors to consider in this section include:

- How can pedagogical activities be designed to encourage compassion from students?
- How could student success with compassion be measured?

5.5.4 Power

Power is the final component of PPCP. Whereas the first three components—people, place and compassion—are directed by the educator, this final component is driven by the student. Power is the student response to the previous three components. It may be asked why this component is 'power' rather than 'empower'. Empower can be defined as 'to give someone official authority or the freedom to do something' (Cambridge Dictionary 2023). This suggests that teachers have some form of control over the student by allowing them to undertake specific tasks or giving them the necessary skills. I would argue that empower is not the suitable terminology to use for several reasons. Firstly, the students already have the necessary abilities to undertake tasks. They have achieved highly in their previous studies and gained entry to study at an educational institute in a language that is not their own. Secondly, 'empower' suggests that teachers are taking an authoritative approach to decide when, where and how students should express themselves. It suggests that teachers are the gatekeepers with the students needing to impress in order to obtain the pass key. In a humanistic approach to pedagogy, teachers are the facilitators who nurture the learner to their potential rather than constructing their outcomes, thus 'power' is the name of this component. As EAP practitioners we often take the stance that learners are in deficit and need significant scaffolding to achieve desired outcomes. We do not give students credit for what they are already capable and have knowledge of. By providing learners with favourable learning conditions, they have that opportunity to show their existing and potential skills. As stated in Sect. 4.1, many EAP learners are academically ready for disciplinary studies (Hu and Trenkic 2019) so if we provide them with opportunities to show them we can give them the power to develop their own learning.

5.6 Summarising PPCP

This chapter has presented PPCP, its creation, visualisation and its individual components. It has made suggestions on how practitioners can apply the theory to their work. However, before concluding this chapter it could be considered pertinent to demonstrate how PPCP aligns to the humanistic PTAs outlined in Chapter 2. This is illustrated by Table 5.2 which lists each of the PTAs and their link to either people, place or compassion. Power is not included by the table as this is an outcome determined by the student and this will vary by student. The table demonstrates that each of the individual PTAs is linked to at least one of people, place and compassion. PPCP differs in that it collectivises these PTAs to provide a more all-round method to humanistic educational approaches.

Table 5.2 PTAs and PPCP connections

	People	Place	Compassion
Montessori's method		x	x
Maslow's hierarchy of needs	x		
Rogers' student-centred learning	x		
Affective learning			x
Aloni's principles for humanistic pedagogy	x		
Csikszentmihalyi's theory of flow			x
Motivation	x		
Pekrun's achievement emotions			x
Positive education			x
Stevick's elements of humanism			x
Sustainable learning	x		x
TBL	x		
Vygotsky's SCT	x		
Gattegno's SW	x		x
Lozanov's Suggestopedia		x	

References

Abbas, Jawad. 2020. Service quality in higher education institutions: Qualitative evidence from the students' perspectives using Maslow hierarchy of needs. *International Journal of Quality and Service Sciences* 12 (3): 371–384. https://doi.org/10.1108/IJQSS-02-2020-0016.

An, Jiangshan, and Nathan Thomas. 2021. Students' beliefs about the role of interaction for science learning and language learning in EMI science classes: Evidence from high schools in China. *Linguistics and Education* 65: 100972. https://doi.org/10.1016/j.linged.2021.100972.

Baars, S., G. L. M. Schellings, J. P. Joore, and P. J. V. van Wesemael. 2023. Physical learning environments' supportiveness to innovative pedagogies: Students' and teachers' experiences. *Learning Environments Research* 26 (2): 617–659. https://doi.org/10.1007/s10984-022-09433-x.

Beard, Karen Stansberry. 2015. Theoretically speaking: An Interview with Mihaly Csikszentmihalyi on flow theory development and its usefulness in addressing contemporary Challenges in Education. *Educational Psychology Review* 27 (2): 353–364. https://www.jstor.org/stable/43548480.

Biwer, Felicitas, Wisnu Wiradhany, Mirjam oude Egbrink, Harm Hospers, Stella Wasenitz, Walter Jansen, and Anique de Bruin A. 2021. Changes and adaptations: how university students self-regulate their online learning during the COVID-19 pandemic. *Frontiers in Psychology* 12: 642593. https://doi.org/10.3389/fpsyg.2021.642593.

Breiby, Monica Adele, Åshild Lappegard Hauge, Stig Holen, and Trygve Stølan. 2023. The students like me less in digital lectures: teachers' experiences of teaching in digital learning environments with large groups of students. During the COVID-19 pandemic. *Seminar.net—Media, Technology and Lifelong Learning* 19 (2). https://doi.org/10.7577/seminar.5503.

Cambridge Dictionary. 2023. https://dictionary.cambridge.org/dictionary/english/empower. Accessed on 26 July 2024.

Canterbury Christ Church University. 2024. What is compassionate pedagogy? https://www.canterbury.ac.uk/learning-and-teaching-enhancement/resources-for-academics/Compassionate-Pedagogy/What-is-Compassionate-Pedagogy.aspx#:~:text=%E2%80%98Compassionate%20Pedagogy%E2%80%99%20is%20about%20creating%20a%20learning%20environment,actively%20seeks%20to%20reduce%20these%20barriers%20to%20learning. Accessed on 15 July 2024.

Cleveland, Benjamin, and Kenn Fisher. 2014. The evaluation of physical learning environments: A critical review of the literature. *Learning Environments Research* 17: 1–28. https://doi.org/10.1007/s10984-013-9149-3.

Clifton, Jonathan. 2006. Facilitator talk. *ELT Journal* 60 (2): 142–150. https://doi.org/10.1093/elt/cci101.

Cornelius-White, Jeffrey. 2007. Learner-centred teacher-student relationships are effective: A meta analysis. *Review of Educational Research* 77 (1): 113–143. https://doi.org/10.3102/003465430298563.

Dillenbourg, Pierre. 2013. Design for classroom orchestration. *Computers and education* 69:485–492. https://doi.org/10.1016/j.compedu.2013.04.013.

Dörnyei, Zoltán, and Tim Murphey. 2003. *Group dynamics in the language classroom.* Cambridge: Cambridge University Press.

Dörrenbächer, Laura, and Franziska Perels. 2016. Self-regulated learning profiles in college students: Their relationship to achievement, personality, and the effectiveness of an intervention to foster self-regulated learning. *Learning and Individual Differences* 51: 229–241. https://doi.org/10.1016/j.lindif.2016.09.015.

Dyer, Laura. 2021. The pedagogical panic—from interruption to progress: reflecting on creativity under pressure. https://celt.leeds.ac.uk/the-pedagogical-panic-from-interruption-to-progress-reflecting-on-creativity-under-pressure/. Accessed on 21 December 2023.

Edmondson, Amy. 1999. Psychological safety and learning behavior in work teams. *Administrative Science Quarterly* 44 (2): 350–383. https://doi.org/10.2307/2666999.

Ellis, R. A., and P. Goodyear. 2016. Models of learning space: Integrating research on space, place and learning in higher education. *Review of Education* 4 (2): 149–191. https://doi.org/10.1002/rev3.3056.

Feng, L. 2024. Modeling the contribution of EFL students' digital literacy to their foreign language enjoyment and self-efficacy in online education. *The Asia-Pacific Education Researcher* 33 (4): 977–985. https://doi.org/10.1007/s40299-023-00787-1.

Fernández Dobao, Ana. 2012. Collaborative writing tasks in the L2 classroom: Comparing group, pair, and individual work. *Journal of Second Language Writing* 21 (1): 40–58. https://doi.org/10.1016/j.jslw.2011.12.002.

Fernández Dobao, Ana. 2014. Vocabulary learning in collaborative tasks: a comparison of pair and small group work. *Language Teaching Research* 18 (4): 497–520. https://doi.org/10.1177/1362168813519730.

Gabbard, Glen O. 2000. Disguise or consent: problems and recommendations concerning the publication and presentation of clinical material. *International journal of psychoanalysis* 81: 1071–1086. https://www.ipa.world/IPA/IPA_DOCS/PDFDocuments/Confidentiality%20Committee%20Background%20Reading/Gabbard%20(2000)%20Disguise%20or%20Consent.pdf.

Gilbert, Theo. 2016a. *Assess compassion in higher education? Why and how could we do that?* LINK. University of Hertfordshire. https://www.herts.ac.uk/link/volume-2,-issue-1/assess-compassion-in-higher-education-how-and-why-would-we-do-that.

Gilbert, Theo. 2016b. Embedding and assessing compassion in the university curriculum. *The international academic forum. The European Conference on Education 2016 Official Conference Proceedings*, 77–88. https://uhra.herts.ac.uk/id/eprint/13926/2/ECE2016_proceedings.pdf.

Grier, Francis. 2023. Anonymisation. *The International Journal of Psychoanalysis* 104 (6): 981–985. https://doi.org/10.1080/00207578.2023.2286763.

Han, Ye, and Fiona Hyland. 2019. Academic emotions in written corrective feedback situations. *Journal of English for Academic Purposes* 38: 1–13. https://doi.org/10.1016/j.jeap.2018.12.003.

Heron, Marion, and Joanne Webster. 2019. Scaffolding talk in EAP lessons: An examination of experienced teachers' practices. *Innovation in Language Learning and Teaching* 13 (4): 358–370. https://doi.org/10.1080/17501229.2018.1466892.

Hu, Ruolin, and Danijela Trenkic. 2019. The effects of coaching and repeated test-taking on Chinese candidates' IELTS scores, their English proficiency, and subsequent academic achievement. *International Journal of Bilingual Education and Bilingualism* 24 (10): 1486–1501. https://doi.org/10.1080/13670050.2019.1691498.

Islam, Md. Shaiful, and Mahani Bt Stapa. 2021. Students' low proficiency in spoken English in private universities in Bangladesh: reasons and remedies. *Language Testing in Asia* 11 (1): 1–31. https://doi.org/10.1186/s40468-021-00139-0.

Li, Jia, and Lillian Mak. 2022. The effects of using an online collaboration tool on college students' learning of academic writing skills. *System* 105: 102712. https://doi.org/10.1016/j.system.2021.102712.

Long, M. H. 1996. The role of linguistic environment in second language acquisition. In *Handbook of second language acquisition,* eds. William C Ritchie and Tej K. Bhatia, 413–468. San Diego: Academic Press.

Long, Michael H. 1981. Input, interaction and second-language acquisition. *Native Language and Foreign Language Acquisition* 379 (1): 259–278. https://doi.org/10.1111/j.1749-6632.1981.tb42014.x.

Low, Setha. 2016. *Spatializing culture: The ethnography of space and place.* London: Routledge.

Lwin, Soe Marlar, Christine Goh, and Paul Doyle. 2012. "I'm going to split you all up": examining transitions to group/pair work in two primary English classrooms. *Language and Education* 26 (1): 19–33. https://doi.org/10.1080/09500782.2011.609281.

MacIntyre, Peter, and Tammy Gregersen. 2012. Emotions that facilitate language learning: the positive-broadening power of the imagination. *Studies in Second Language Learning and Teaching* 2 (2): 193–1. https://doi.org/10.14746/ssllt.2012.2.2.4.

Maratos, Frances A., Paul Gilbert, and Theo Gilbert. 2019. Improving well-being in higher education: Adopting a compassionate approach. In *Values of the university in times of uncertainty*, ed. Paul Gibbs, Jill Jameson, and Alex Elwick, 261–278. Cham: Springer.

Marmot, Alexi. 2014. Managing the campus facility management and design, the student experience and university effectiveness. In *The physical university: contours of space and place in higher education,* ed. Paul Temple. London: Routledge. https://doi.org/10.4324/9781315813776-5.

Maxwell, Bruce. 2017. Pursuing the aim of compassionate empathy in higher education. In *The pedagogy of compassion at the heart of higher education*, ed. Paul Gibbs, 33–49. Cham: Springer.

Morán-Soto, Gustavo, Aradaryn Marsh, Omar Israel González. Peña, Matthew Sheppard, José Isabel. Gómez-Quiñones, and Lisa C. Benson. 2022. Effect of the COVID-19 pandemic on the sense of belonging in higher education for STEM students in the United States and Mexico. *Sustainability* 14 (24): 16627. https://doi.org/10.3390/su142416627.

OECD. 2015. OECD Education 2030 Incheon Declaration: Towards Inclusive an Equitable Quality Education and lifelong learning for all. https://uis.unesco.org/sites/default/files/documents/education-2030-incheon-framework-for-action-implementation-of-sdg4-2016-en_2.pdf. Accessed on 19 April 2024

Oleson, Kathryn C. 2023. *Promoting inclusive classroom dynamics in higher education: A research-based pedagogical guide for faculty*. Abingdon: Routledge.

Palincsar, A. Sullivan. 1998. Social constructivist perspectives on teaching and learning. *Annual Review of Psychology* 49: 345–375. https://doi.org/10.1146/annurev.psych.49.1.345.

Peng, Lei, Shitao Jin, Yuan Deng, and Yichen Gong. 2022. Students' perceptions of active learning classrooms from an informal learning perspective: Building a full-time sustainable learning environment in higher education. *Sustainability* 14: 8578. https://doi.org/10.3390/su14148578.

Phirangee, Krystle, and Jim Hewitt. 2024. Enhancing learners' sense of belonging in online threaded discussions. *Distance Education* 1–21. https://doi.org/10.1080/01587919.2024.2375289.

Prabhavathy, P., and S.N. Mahalakshmi. 2012. ELT with specific regard to humanistic approach. *Journal of Humanities and Social Sciences* 1 (1): 38–39. https://www.iosrjournals.org/iosr-jhss/papers/vol1-issue1/G0113839.pdf.

Qi, Jiaming. 2024. Analyzing the time-series relationship between learning atmosphere, negative emotions, and academic engagement in language learners. *Innovation in Language Learning and Teaching* 1–18. https://doi.org/10.1080/17501229.2024.2444645.

Raettig, Tim, and Ulrich Weger. 2018. Learning as a shared peak experience: Interactive flow in higher education. *International Journal of Applied Positive Psychology* 2: 39–60. https://doi.org/10.1007/s41042-018-0011-9.

Riazi, A. Mehdi., Hessameddin Ghanbar, and Ismaeil Fazel. 2020. The contexts, theoretical and methodological orientation of EAP research: Evidence from empirical articles published in the Journal of English for Academic Purposes. *Journal of English for Academic Purposes* 48: 100925. https://doi.org/10.1016/j.jeap.2020.100925.

Rice, Mary, and Michael Dunn. 2023. Inclusive online and distance education for learners with dis/abilities. In *Inclusive online and distance education for learners with dis/abilities. Promoting accessibility and equity*, eds. Mary Rice and Michael Dunn, 1–6. Abingdon: Routledge.

Shahjahan, Riyad A. 2014. Being 'lazy' and slowing down: toward decolonizing time, our body, and pedagogy. *Educational Philosophy and Theory* 47 (5): 488–501. https://doi.org/10.1080/00131857.2014.880645.

Thanh, Pham Ti Hong, and Robin Gillies. 2010. Designing a culturally appropriate format of formative peer assessment for Asian students: the case of Vietnamese students. *International Journal of Educational Reform* 19 (2): 72–85. https://doi.org/10.1177/105678791001900201.

Turnbull, David. 2002. Performance and narrative, bodies and movement in the construction of places and objects, spaces and knowledges: The case of the Maltese megaliths. *Theory, Culture and Society* 19 (5–6): 125–143.

Waddington, Kathryn. 2016. The compassion gap in UK universities. *International Practice Development Journal* 6 (1): 10. https://doi.org/10.19043/ipdj.61.010.

Waddington, Kathryn, and Bryan Bonaparte. 2025. Compassion in higher education: Fashion or future for relational pedagogies? *Higher Education Research and Development* 44 (3): 785–792. https://doi.org/10.1080/07294360.2024.2406505.

Wake, Stephanie, Madeleine Pownall, Richard Harris, and Pam Birtill. 2023. Balancing pedagogical innovation with psychological safety? Student perceptions of authentic assessment. *Assessment and Evaluation in Higher Education* 49 (4): 511–522. https://doi.org/10.1080/02602938.2023.2275519.

Wallace, Susan. 2015. *A dictionary of education*, 2nd ed. Oxford: Oxford University Press.

Weddell, Martin, and Angi Malderez. 2013. *Understanding language classroom contexts: The starting point for change*. New York: Bloomsbury.

Zembylas, Michalinos. 2017. In search of critical and strategic pedagogies of compassion: Interrogating pity and sentimentality in higher education. In *The pedagogy of compassion at the heart of higher education*, ed. Paul Gibbs, 173–188. Cham: Springer.

6

Compendium of Activities

6.1 Overview and Outline of Activities

In the preceding chapter I introduced PPCP, its origins and explored its components. In this chapter I demonstrate the application of the theory through a compendium of pedagogical activities which reflect PPCP in their designing and planning. The activities were selected by asking myself the following two questions:

- What aspects of EAP are generally considered more challenging for my learners?
- How can I facilitate the EAP learning experience?

From these questions I present eight pedagogical activities that developed as a direct result of PPCP or are linked strongly to the theory and individually address areas that specific aspects that could foster the overall EAP learning experience.

Activity Presentation

L. Dyer, *A Humanistic Approach to English for Academic Purposes Pedagogy*,
https://doi.org/10.1007/978-3-032-00186-3_6

The eight activities in this compendium are listed in alphabetical order. Each activity is linked to the three purposes of EAP outlined in Sect. 1. 3 which are:

A. Bridging the perceived language gap of what is considered a language deficit between completed studies and future studies in the English language.
B. Raising consciousness and fostering the designated skills deemed necessary for academic study.
C. Raising awareness of community skills.

Each activity may link to one, two or all three of the purposes of EAP. All activity outlines in this compendium use the following structure:

Rationale and discussion—explaining the choice of topic and relevant literature surrounding it.
Link the activity to the purposes of EAP—this section states which of purposes of EAP outlined in Sect. 1.3.
Applying PPCP—this section considers the people, place, compassion and power of the activity.
Procedure—an explanation of how to set up the activity.

As a practitioner you can choose whether or not to carry out the activities as they are described or to make adaptations to suit their learners. It is hoped that the activities will inspire practitioners to undertake their own explorations of PPCP and how to apply it to their own teaching practices.

The eight activities outlined in this compendium are:

- academic studies exploration
- conversation sessions
- dialogic presentation
- intercultural rhetoric as a foundation
- learner vs. AI
- listening tag team
- paired peer feedback
- students teach students

Note: several of the activities state that the 'place' component should be a comfortable environment conducive to learning. It is for you as the practitioner to decide how to manage this aspect with Sects. 5.5.2 and 5.5.3 serving as potential aids to this.

6.2 Academic Studies Exploration

Rationale and Discussion

The purpose of PSPs are to serve as a pathway for future academic studies in the English language. Whilst many of the skills and language needs that are predicted to be useful for future study are covered in these courses, there often remains a gap where learners have the opportunity to visualise how the content of PSPs can be applied to their future endeavours. In this academic studies exploration, learners explore aspects of their chosen academic programme in order to understand what is expected of them. This activity encourages exploration of aspects of the programme such as module selection, assessment and reading lists. This in turn can lead to increased intrinsic motivation to foster learning as curiosity is aroused as well as the potential to reduce negative emotions around uncertainty and purpose (Silvia 2019). It can also produce conditions for learners to visualise the ideal self (Dörnyei 2009) through conducting academic studies in the English language.

Exploration is one activity that can develop learner growth and independence (Al-Obaydi 2021). A humanistic approach emphasises the importance of discovery learning and the learner's just needs for self-determination (Wallace 2015). It is easier to learn about topics which interest us (Gruber et al. 2014) and as many EAP students are likely to have some form of input in their choice of academic studies, this is an area that can be exploited in learning processes. This is also an opportunity for the commencement of academic acculturation (Stoller 1999) that learners would likely need to be familiar with for their academic studies. It can also remove them temporarily from the EAP bubble (see Sect. 4.5.2.2) in which they may feel comfortable. The academic studies exploration is designed to be an informative and motivating task for the learner which allows them to see their ideal self—one who is successfully able to carry out their academic studies in the English language.

Link to Purposes **of EAP**

The academic studies exploration applies reading skills in its first stage and with the second stage skills dependent on the chosen output. This activity addresses purpose B of the purposes of EAP in that it raises awareness of the skills students require in order to undertake academic studies.

Applying PPCP

People: students work independently on their exploration before sharing their findings with others. Alternatively place students with others who may have the same academic studies pathway and encourage a joint exploration.
Place: a location comfortable and conducive to the activity where students can work independently before sharing their discoveries.
Compassion: students gain an understanding of the relevance of their EAP studies in assisting their preparation for their future academic studies.
Power: motivation may increase as interest is garnered through focusing on the end goal of progressing to or building awareness of academic studies.

Procedure

Set students the task of individually researching their future study programme or a specific aspect such as assessment or one module.

Students produce output demonstrating their understanding of their academic studies programme and making links to their EAP course. The output could be written, verbal or visual with an intended audience of either teachers, peers or both. One possible output is a dialogic presentation (see Sect. 6.4).

6.3 Conversation Sessions

Rationale

It is recognised that much focus of EAP courses is on the skills of reading and writing with less emphasis on listening and speaking (Dippold et al. 2019). Yet some learners may have limited opportunity for speaking in their previous learning (Akazaki 2010) which could lead to lower speaking confidence. Although there is a vast array of publications aimed at learners to help them 'speak confidently', the real-life application and experience of speaking often does not reflect what learners expect. By introducing increased speaking opportunities within an EAP course, learners will have the chance to increase their speaking confidence. These speaking opportunities should be less structured, for example not spoon feeding students with a list of questions to ask. This is because structured conversation restricts students to language deemed necessary to complete tasks, but a free conversation allows students to incorporate this into their existing language base (Howatt and Widdowson 2004 cited by Rubdy 2005). Language is a tool for developing, enlarging and maintaining social networks (Conein 2011) and in this instance as learners are preparing for entry to academic study in English these social networks could include peers, educators, personal tutors, professional services staff and technical services staff. It is recognised that former PSP students may struggle with unstructured speaking (Dippold et al. 2019) therefore these conversation sessions aim to build up speaking confidence to aid EAP students in their speaking during their academic studies to give them the best opportunity to succeed (Dippold et al. 2019).

Link to Purposes of EAP

Conversation sessions is a valuable activity for learners and it addresses each of the three purposes of EAP. Through conversation sessions learners have the opportunity to put into practice their existing and recently acquired language skills alongside developing communication skills. These sessions can also be used to raise awareness of the need for speaking for community skills.

Applying PPCP

People: students should be in small groups to allow for each member to have the opportunity to participate
Place: the environment should be comfortable
Compassion: allow for students to control the discussion. Error correction should be avoided unless the errors are impeding
Power: students lead and control the direction of the conversation, allowing for them to develop confidence and fluency

Procedure

Place students in small groups of 3–4.
Set students a task relevant to their EAP or academic studies.
Guiding points or questions may be provided but should be kept to a minimum to enable students to direct the conversation.

6.4 Dialogic Presentation

Rationale and Discussion

In recent years there has been an increasing amount of importance of spoken academic communication, one method of which is through presentations (Hyland 2006 and Lee 2016 cited in Hu and Liu 2018). Presentations can be challenging for both L1 and perhaps more so non-L1 speakers of a language (Ducasse and Brown 2023) as the non-L1 speaker attempts to present their information in comprehensible language whilst demonstrating the ability to think critically, adhere to local academic rhetorical conventions, navigate academic content as well as the presentation performance itself (Ducasse and Brown 2023). For the EAP student there is the further component of completing the task in a foreign language (Mumford 2018). Success in a presentation task itself may be further compounded by students lacking previous experience in the activity (Bankowski 2010) and adapting to the Western approach to teaching where the learner is actively involved (Arthur

1997 cited in Bankowski 2010). Feelings of anxiety, fear, shyness and low confidence in speaking ability can also impact on presentation success (Kittiyano 2020). Additionally, the use of strict time restrictions may lead to students feeling pressured to orally produce their research within a short period of time within a single take. Audience questions may also be prepared in advance leading to rehearsed answers, often leading to teachers taking control. All of these issues can compound a learner's performance and be detrimental to overall outcomes. Presentations are integral to the majority of EAP courses (Bankowski 2010) and are widely used as assessment. However, despite the summative importance placed on presentations, training on this aspect of communication remains less of a priority than written discourse. As a result, a student who may be considered as a successful learner of written English may not produce a presentation representative of their true academic ability (Kittiyano 2020). The dialogic presentation is a learner-centred form of presenting through a less anxiety inducing and a more inclusive learning environment (Dyer 2023, 2024). Throughout the activity learners are encouraged to collaborate through negotiating with and supporting the presenter through dialogue. This provides opportunity for presenters to demonstrate their knowledge beyond what might be in a monologic presentation. Dialogue is an essential factor in the language learning process (Basturkmen 2016) and this activity allows students to demonstrate that they can talk with people rather than at them.

Link to Purposes of EAP

The dialogic presentation is an activity that has been adapted from a traditional monologic presentation by applying PPCP. In its role as a presentation, the dialogic presentation addresses purpose B in the purpose of EAP which is to raise awareness of and foster the skills for academic study.

Applying PPCP

People: limit the audience size to increase engagement between them and the presenter.

Place: allow the presentation to be carried out in a more psychologically safe location than standing in front of a large group.
Compassion: allowing the audience to partake in the discussion could help to support the presenter and develop their work further.
Power: students feel more confident when speaking in front of the smaller audience in a comfortable environment.

Procedure

Students should prepare a piece of work as if they will carry out a monologic presentation.
Put students in small groups of 4–5.
Create a comfortable environment for both speaker and audience such as sitting around a table.
Presenter displays presentation on laptop and 'talks' about it rather than presenting.
Group members question and highlight points they see during the presentation. They are free to do this at any point during the activity.
Give students no strict individual time limit but you may wish to give an overall group time limit such as 1 hour with students managing their own individual times.

6.5 Intercultural Rhetoric as a Foundation

Rationale and Discussion

Intercultural rhetoric developed from contrastive rhetoric which is the study of written discourse, its similarities and differences between individuals from different cultural backgrounds (Connor 2011 cited by Connor et al. 2016). This compendium activity builds upon the concept of contrastive rhetoric, first put forward by Kaplan in 1966 (Connor 1996), which is collocated with the Council of Europe's (2021) CEFR. It also coordinates with BALEAP's Can Do Framework (BALEAP, n.d.). Contrastive rhetoric proposes that each language has its own conventions and discourse patterns (Connor 1996), and that these can impact on a second language when presenting information. It would be fair to say that contrastive rhetoric is a concept that focuses on the negatives as it considers transfer from first to second to be an interference and hindrance. It does not consider why or how the learner may transfer discourse or language patterns from their first language. Subsequently, the term intercultural rhetoric was developed to consider the positives that there may be in comparing rhetorics (Connor et al. 2016). Supporting the positivity of language acquisition, CEFR uses 'can do' statements which are oriented towards the learner's abilities and knowledge of what they can already do (Faez et al. 2011). CEFR aims to develop skills and acquisition through goal attaining tasks that replicate real world situations (Pica 2008, cited in Faez et al. 2011), giving learners a sense of achievement and motivation to use language in situations that normally they would not (Faez et al. 2011).

This activity combines intercultural rhetorics in the students' L1 and the English language with the CEFR to highlight the positives in what learners can already do via the following:

- Transfer from L1 or existing skillset to English
- What they already know about or are aware of
- Areas to learn

This translanguaging or trans-rhetorical activity allows learners to use their own existing knowledge and experience in developing their EAP, as opposed to the 'clean slate' approach that EAP courses may take. It could lead to reductions in time spent on some aspects of EAP if it is discovered that learners already have some knowledge or awareness of them, allowing for time to be reallocated to other areas. Much instruction on EAP pedagogical tasks focuses on the mechanistic step by step processes that learners should go through in order to produce the desired outcome. In contrast, this approach asks the learner to review what they already know and build upon, modify or add to this existing knowledge. The activity focuses on positive existing attributes and pitches the level higher through analysis of the student's own work. Collaboration is encouraged through the sharing of existing rhetorics and developing of the target one.

Link to Purposes of EAP

This activity links to purpose A in the purposes of EAP due to its language based focus.

Applying PPCP

People: allow learners to work together to discover how their L1 and previous learning experience can support their EAP studies.
Place: allow activity to place in an environment that fosters sharing and collaboration.
Compassion: allow learners to use their existing knowledge to develop their English language and academic skills.
Power: learners have the potential to speed up language and academic skills acquisition through bypassing areas that they can already complete successfully.

Procedure

There are several options available to commence this task:

1. Set the same writing task for all students such as a needs analysis essay at the commencement of the course
   OR
2. Students bring in a piece of writing from their previous studies which has been translated into English. As this is not an assessment this translation can be done through an app or website.

Place students in small groups of 3 or 4

Ask students to share their writing and talk through the type of information they included, where they got it from, how it is presented and the structure of the piece of writing (along the lines of a genre analysis).
Students should compare similarities and differences between their written work.

Ask students to consider what elements of their written work could also be used in their current EAP setting such as the use of references, paragraph structure and so on.
Ask groups to consider if there are any extra elements they think they may need for their EAP and future academic course.
Groups compile a list: *what we can already do*, *what we know about*, a *goal to learn.*
Highlight the positives. Ask students to show what they already know and that it can be transferred into their EAP learning. They should also consider what is different but they feel they could do successfully.
Ask students to create personal list of what they may need to learn.

6.6 Learner vs. AI

Rationale and Discussion

At the time of writing AI is rapidly expanding across the educational sector. Whilst AI has been positively received in wider society, the education sector is one area which has raised concerns about the use of AI, citing academic malpractice as one of the determining factors (Barrett and Pack 2023). However, advocates of AI state that the technology can be beneficial, especially if learners are made aware of its limitations (Godwin-Jones 2022; Tseng and Warschauer 2023). Whilst research has shown that AI may be able to produce high quality written work in some areas that can be rated higher than that of human output, others may be lacking comparison (Herbold et al. 2023). It has been noted that although AI's linguistic outputs may be considered grammatically, syntactically and coherently accurate, these may not satisfy the requirements of a written task. For example, AI may not provide the correct referencing system or fulfil the use of epistemic markers (Herbold et al. 2023). AI may also produce evaluations and conclusions that are not representative of the user's opinions, instead taking a more neutral stance and having lower levels of bias (Guo et al. 2023). This learner vs. AI activity takes a positive approach to the use of AI and asks students to consider its limitations in producing a piece of academic writing.

Link to Purposes of EAP

This activity addresses A and B of the purposes of EAP through its analysis of the language and textuality of the AI generated product alongside the skills of navigating AI in academia.

Applying PPCP

People: this task requires both human and non-human participants. Human participants work together in a pair or small group and they are pitted against the non-human.

Place: the activity takes place through AI writing generating software and a conducive collaborative learning environment.

Compassion: allowing students to work in pairs or groups allows some anonymisation if they find the task challenging.

Power: students have the opportunity to test themselves against AI, showing what they have learnt in their EAP studies and a sense of achievement in beating the non-human.

Procedure

Set a written task such as an essay on a topic that can be considered accessible to your students.

Put an essay question into AI software to generate an essay. It is a good idea to do this in front of the students so that they can see capabilities of AI. Give students access to the AI generated essay. Alternatively ask students to use AI themselves to generate the essay.

Place students in pairs or small groups

Ask students to work together to correct, improve or make changes to the AI generated essay using their EAP skills.

Students share their work with the class

Students reflect on the positives of AI and how they used their EAP skills to challenge it.

6.7 Listening Tag Team

Rationale and Discussion

Lectures have become the most widely used mode of instruction in tertiary education (Rahimirad and Moini 2015) but can be challenging for L1 and non-L1 speakers alike (Selamat and Sidhu 2013). EAP listeners require an additional skill level in that there is the challenge of decoding content in another language whilst checking for gaps in knowledge, taking notes, understanding visuals, noting what is and is not important information through lexicogrammatical markers (Deroey and Taverniers 2012), participating in lecture either through discussions or questions plus maintaining concentration for the duration of the lecture (Rahimirad and Moini 2015; Field 2011; Ferris and Tagg 1996). Through all of this the listener must create a mental representation of the oral communication in order to gain an understanding of its content (Rodgers and Webb 2016) and maintain this construction throughout the lecture which may last for several hours. Yet listening to lectures remains a key component of academic study and in order to be successful in an academic institution a good level of listening ability is required (Rahimirad and Moini 2015). Due to the wide range of challenges an EAP learner may face in listening, the listening tag team is suggested as a possible aid through sharing the intensive listening responsibilities in longer listening activities such as lectures. The listening tag team is a collaborative and supportive approach to listening to lectures. It is an approach that can be carried forward and applied by learners to lectures in their academic studies.

Link to Purposes of EAP

The activity covers EAP purpose A as it raises awareness of discourse markers, signally and transitions in lectures and other extended listening activities. It is also linked to purpose B as it highlights the key skill of listening which deemed necessary for academic study.

Applying PPCP

People: allow students to undertake listening tasks collaboratively.

Place: all students working together should be in the same location so that the main listener can take up their role.
Compassion: allow for students to experience distractions, interruptions and multitasking whilst carrying out periods of intense listening.
Power: students gain a more in depth understanding of lectures through the short bursts of intensive listening.

Procedure

Before the lecture

- Students work with a pair or small group
- Students read through and prepare for the lecture together by discussing and researching key points on lecture materials*
- Each group member selects a different part of the lecture to focus on

*In an ideal situation information would be available prior to the lecture. However, if this is not the case, students could each plan to carry out 20 minutes consecutive slots of intensive listening.

During the lecture

- Students listen in detail to their allocated section of the lecture
- Once that section is completed, students should signal to their group member to take over the listening
- When not undertaking their main listening task(s), students could continue to listen extensively or other choose not to listen at all

After the lecture

- Students collocate their notes and discuss together the content of the lecture, sharing opinions, thinking critically and considering areas for further research.

6.8 Paired Peer Feedback

Rationale and Discussion

Peer feedback is viewed as being a beneficial learning tool yet it is not one that is widely used (Adachi et al. 2018), nor is it viewed positively by learners (McGarr and Clifford 2013). By nature, peer feedback means no teacher input into feedback content which means that it is up to students to take control and become the 'expert' with their feedback comments (McGarr and Clifford 2013). However, learners may not feel confident or comfortable enough to individually comment on the work of others. To resolve this, working with a peer to generate feedback can help with motivation (Hiromori et al. 2021). Additionally, maintaining comment anonymity encourages a more positive attitude to the task and makes participants more likely to respond (Ge 2019; Chuaphalakit et al. 2019; Coté 2014). This peer feedback task uses both pair work and anonymity to allow learners to take control of feedback generation whilst demonstrating criticality and collaboration skills (Dyer 2021).

Link to Purposes of EAP

Paired peer feedback is an adaptation of the traditional approach to peer feedback which normally takes the form of individuals generating feedback for others. This activity covers point B of the purpose of EAP through its requirement for providing and responding to feedback.

Applying PPCP

People: allow students to work together to develop peer feedback
Place: the generation of feedback should happen in a place where students feel comfortable talking about the work of others. There should also be a place for students to record their feedback and for the receivers to view it
Compassion: allow for anonymity or semi-anonymity to increase student confidence in providing feedback
Power: students take control and become the 'experts' who assess their peers

Procedure

- Prior to giving peer feedback

Students should individually produce a piece of work that will be given peer feedback

- The feedback task

Introduce peer feedback to the students, asking them to consider its purpose and what they would expect to see in feedback.

Place students in pairs, instructing them that they will work together to produce feedback for two other students in the class. Depending on the amount of scaffolding needed, at this point you may decide to provide pairs with criteria to use when giving feedback, or you may wish to leave students to their own devices.

Pairs view both pieces of work they need to give feedback on. They should share opinions and ideas for what feedback they would give to both items, ideally in a confidential location. In an online context this could be done in a private breakout room. In face-to-face teaching this activity could be undertaken outside the learning environment (such as for homework) or if inside by instructing learners to maintain source anonymity in their discussions.

Students work as a pair to produce feedback for both pieces of work.
Teacher separates pairs.
Students produce their peer feedback, based upon what was discussed with their partner.
Feedback should ideally be recorded somewhere anonymously.
It is recommended that teachers should check feedback once it has been submitted.

- After giving peer feedback.

Students read and consider the feedback they have received from their peers.

6.9 Students Teach Students

Rationale and Discussion

A key constituent in humanistic education is the abandonment of authoritarian processes to allow for personal self-actualisation (Krikorian 2023). One method to achieve this is to place the student in the role of educator as a means to engage students in teaching and learning practices (Stigmar 2016). Through student-to-student teaching, learners become more aware of the processes of self-reflection, assessment and learning (Stigmar 2016). This in turn can result in positive academic outcomes (Goodlad 1997) and develop the person as a whole which has been highlighted throughout this publication as a key feature of humanistic education. Peer teaching encourages the student to become active in their engagement with others, their own agency and autonomy (Stigmar 2016). The activity itself can also enable learning through the presentation and reception of information (Torshizi and Bahraman 2019). Students as teachers can prove to be more effective instructor than the teacher as the student immerses themselves in their 'lesson' content (Roscoe 2014).

Link to Purposes of EAP

Students teaching students is a longstanding activity which could prove valuable for EAP students. This activity addresses purpose B of the purposes of EAP as it aims to develop skills such as presenting and producing material for a non-specialist audience.

Applying PPCP

People: students as both teacher and learner
Place: allow for the teaching to take place in a comfortable context
Compassion: allow for students to choose their own topic to teach so that they feel comfortable and thus decrease anxiety levels
Power: 'teachers' learn from their experience through a more in depth understanding of the learning process

Procedure

Ask students to choose a topic they would like to teach to their peers. Possibilities could include an academic topic they have studied before or are interested in, their language or culture (if in a multilingual or multicultural cohort) or a topic of general interest. They should produce a small number of activities that will help the learners achieve the stated learning objectives.

Students prepare their 'lesson' outside class.
Students deliver their lesson in the desired mode. Contexts may be altered to support your students such as allowing for the lesson to be delivered in small groups or online via asynchronous learning.
Students reflect on their own 'teaching' process and learning from their peers.

References

6.2 Academic Studies Exploration

Al-Obaydi, Liqaa Habeb. 2021. Humanistic learning elements in a blended learning environment: A study in an EFL teaching context. *Interactive Learning Environments* 31 (5): 3098–3111. https://doi.org/10.1080/10494820.2021.1919717.

Dörnyei, Zoltán. 2009. The L2 motivational self system. In *Motivation, language identity and the L2 self*, ed. Zoltán Dörnyei and Ema Ushioda, 9–42. Bristol: Multilingual Matters.

Gruber, Matthias J., Bernard D. Gelman, and Charan Ranganath. 2014. States of curiosity modulate hippocampus-dependent learning via the dopaminergic circuit. *Neuron* 84 (2): 486–496. https://doi.org/10.1016/j.neuron.2014.08.060.

Silvia, Paul J. 2019. Curiosity and motivation. In *The Oxford handbook of human motivation,* ed. Richard M. Ryan, 156–157. Oxford: Oxford University Press. https://doi.org/10.1093/oxfordhb/9780190666453.013.9.

Stoller, Fredericka L. 1999. Time for change: A hybrid curriculum for EAP programs. *TESOL Journal* 8: 9–13. https://doi.org/10.1002/j.1949-3533.1999.tb00150.x.

Wallace, Susan. 2015. *A dictionary of education*, 2nd ed. Oxford: Oxford University Press.

6.3 Conversation Sessions

Akazaki, Misa. 2010. Negotiating different assumptions: The experience of mature Japanese students in British universities. *Journal of Studies in International Education* 14 (4): 355–370. https://doi.org/10.1177/1028315309334642.

Conein, Bernard. 2011. Gossip, conversation and group size: Language as a bonding mechanism. *Irish Journal of Sociology* 19 (1): 116–131. https://doi.org/10.7227/IJS.19.1.6.

Dippold, Doris, Stephanie Bridges, Sue Eccles, and Emma Mullen. 2019. Taking ELF off the shelf: Developing HE students' speaking skills through a focus on English as a lingua franca. *Linguistics and Education*. 54: 100761. https://doi.org/10.1016/j.linged.2019.100761.

Rubdy, Rani. 2005. Review: A history of English language teaching. *ELT Journal* 59 (2): 180–182. https://doi.org/10.1093/eltj/cci033.

6.4 Dialogic Presentation

Bankowski, Elizabeth. 2010. Developing skills for effective academic presentations in EAP. *International Journal of Teaching and Learning in Higher Education* 22 (2): 187–196. https://www.semanticscholar.org/paper/Developing-Skills-for-Effective-Academic-in-EAP-Bankowski/660ef873787d5370c9c7c80c2cc2a3045ce496cb.

Basturkmen, Helen. 2016. Dialogic interaction. In *The Routledge handbook of English for academic purposes*, eds. Ken Hyland and Philip Shaw, 152–164. Abingdon: Routledge. https://doi.org/10.4324/9781315657455-12.

Ducasse, Ana Maria, and Annie Brown. 2023. Rhetorical relations in university students' presentations. *Journal of English for Academic Purposes* 63: 101251. https://doi.org/10.1016/j.jeap.2023.101251.

Dyer, Laura. 2024. The dialogic presentation as a more compassionate approach. *Journal of Learning Development in Higher Education*. 32. https://doi.org/10.47408/jldhe.vi32.1190.

Dyer, Laura. 2023. The dialogic presentation—An alternative presentation approach to decrease anxiety and increase inclusivity. TIPS Blog. https://studenteddev.leeds.ac.uk/news/the-dialogic-presentation-an-alternative-presentation-approach-to-decrease-anxiety-and-increase-inclusivity/#:~:text=This%20blog%20post%20introduces%20an%20alternative%20to%20the%20traditional. Accessed on 15 December 2023.

Hu, Guangwei, and Yanhua Liu. 2018. Three minute thesis presentations as an academic genre: A cross-disciplinary study of genre moves. *Journal of English for Academic Purposes* 35: 16–30. https://doi.org/10.1016/j.jeap.2018.06.004.

Kittiyano, Phra Natthakit. 2020. A study of English speaking for oral presentation of the Bachelor of Arts fourth year students of Mahachulalongkornrajavidyalaya University Chiang Mai Campus at Muang of Chiang Mai in Thailand. *Language in India* 20 (12): 136–160. http://www.languageinindia.com/dec2020/phraenglishoralthaiuniv.pdf.

Mumford, Simon. 2018. Understanding the challenges of academic presentations for EAP students: An exploratory practice approach. In *Developing language teachers with exploratory practice,* eds. Kenan Dikilitaş and Judith Hanks, 103–117. Cham: Palgrave MacMillan. https://doi.org/10.1007/978-3-319-75735-3_6.

6.5 Intercultural Rhetoric as a Foundation for Tasks

BALEAP. n.d. BALEAP Can Do Framework. https://www.baleap.org/wp-content/uploads/2016/04/Can_Do_Framework__with_sample_activities_April_2013.pdf. Accessed on 18 February 2025.

Connor, Ulla M. 1996. *Contrastive rhetoric cross-cultural aspects of second-language writing*. Cambridge: Cambridge University Press. https://doi.org/10.1017/CBO9781139524599.

Connor, Ulla, Estela Ene, and Ana Traversa. 2016. Intercultural rhetoric. In *The Routledge handbook of English for academic purposes,* eds. Ken Hyland and Philip Shaw, 270–282. Abingdon: Routledge. https://doi.org/10.4324/9781315657455-21.

Council of Europe. 2021. Common European framework of reference for languages: learning, teaching, assessment. Council of Europe. https://www.coe.int/en/web/common-european-framework-reference-languages/.

Faez, Farahnaz, Suzanne Majhanovich, Shelly Taylor, Maureen Smith, and Kelly Crowley. 2011. The power of 'can do' statements: teachers' perceptions of CEFR-informed instruction in French as a second language classrooms in Ontario. *Canadian Journal of Applied Linguistics* 14(2): 1–19. https://files.eric.ed.gov/fulltext/EJ967319.pdf.

6.6 Learner vs. AI

Barrett, Alex, and Austin Pack. 2023. Not quite eye to A.I.: student and teacher perspectives on the use of generative artificial intelligence in the writing process. *International Journal of Educational Technology in Higher Education* 20: 59. https://doi.org/10.1186/s41239-023-00427-0.

Godwin-Jones, Robert. 2022. Partnering with AI: Intelligent writing assistance and instructed language learning. *Language Learning and Technology* 26 (2): 5–24. 10125/73474. https://scholarspace.manoa.hawaii.edu/items/ce0dcba9-073a-472f-a263-868a5653c07d.

Guo, Biyang, Xin Zhang, Ziyuan Wang, Minqi Jiang, Jinran Nie, Yuxuan Ding, Jianwei Yue, and Yupeng Wu. 2023. How close is ChatGP to human experts? Comparison corpus, evaluation and detection. *ArXiv.org*. https://arxiv.org/pdf/2301.07597.

Herbold, Steffen, Annette Hautli-Janisz, Ute Heuer, Zlata Kikteva, and Alexander Trautsch. 2023. A large-scale comparison of human-written versus ChatGPT-generated essays. *Scientific Reports* 13: 18617. https://doi.org/10.1038/s41598-023-45644-9.

Tseng, Waverly, and Mark Warschauer. 2023. AI-writing tools in education: If you can't beat them, join them. *Journal of China Computer-Assisted Language Learning* 3 (2): 258–262. https://doi.org/10.1515/jccall-2023-0008.

6.7 Listening Tag Team

Deroey, Katrien L.B. and Miriam Taverniers. 2012. Just remember this: Lexicogrammatical relevance markers in lectures. *English for Specific Purposes* 31 (4): 221–233. https://doi.org/10.1016/j.esp.2012.05.001.

Ferris Dana, and Tracy Tagg. 1996. Academic listening/speaking tasks for ESL students: Problems, suggestions, and implication. *TESOL Quarterly* 30 (2): 297–320. https://onlinelibrary.wiley.com/doi/abs/10.2307/3588145?msockid=1f1bba3d82f4697a379cae61838e685f.

Field, John. 2011. Into the mind of the academic listener. *Journal of English for Academic Purposes* 10 (2): 102–112. https://doi.org/10.1016/j.jeap.2011.04.002.

Rahimirad, Maryam, and Mohammad Raouf Moini. 2015. The challenges of listening to academic lectures for EAP learners and the impact of metacognition on academic lecture listening comprehension. *SAGE Open* 5 (2). https://doi.org/10.1177/2158244015590609.

Rodgers, Michael P.H., and Stuart Webb. 2016. Listening to lectures. In *The Routledge handbook of English for academic purposes,* eds. Ken Hyland and Philip Shaw, 165–176. Abingdon: Routledge. https://doi.org/10.4324/9781315657455.

Selamat, Suzanah, and Sidhu, Gurnam Kaur. 2013. Enhancing listening comprehension: the role of metacognitive strategy instruction (MetSI). *Procedia, Social and Behavioral Sciences.* 90: 421–430. https://doi.org/10.1016/j.sbspro.2013.07.111.

6.8 Paired Peer Feedback

Adachi, Chie, Joanna Hong-Meng Tai, and Philip Dawson. 2018. Academics' perceptions of the benefits and challenges of self and peer assessment in higher education. *Assessment and Evaluation in Higher Education* 43 (2): 294–306. https://doi.org/10.1080/02602938.2017.1339775.

Chuaphalakit, Ken, Inpin Bhornsawan and Prarthana Coffin. 2019. A study of the quality of feedback via the Google classroom-mediated-anonymous online peer feedback activity in a Thai EFL writing classroom. *International Journal of Progressive Education* 15 (5), 103–118. https://eric.ed.gov/?id=EJ1232510.

Coté, Robert A. 2014. Peer feedback in anonymous peer review in an EFL writing class in Spain. *GIST Education and Learning Research Journal* 9: 67–87. https://eric.ed.gov/?id=EJ1062639.

Dyer, Laura. 2021. Generating constructive peer feedback in breakout rooms, TIPS Blog. https://studenteddev.leeds.ac.uk/news/generating-constructive-peer-feedback-in-breakout-rooms/#:~:text=This%20article%20suggests%20a%20method%20for%20improving%20student. Accessed on 25 August 2021.

Ge, Zi-Gang. 2019. Exploring the effect of video feedback from unknown peers on e-learners' English-Chinese translation performance. *Computer Assisted Language Learning* 35 (1–2): 169–189. https://doi.org/10.1080/09588221.2019.1677721.

Hiromori, Tomohito, Masahiro Yoshimura, Makoto Mitsugi, and Ryo Kirimura. 2021. Watch your partner's ehaviors: motivation contagion in L2 pair work. *Journal of Pan-Pacific Association of Applied Linguistics* 25 (1): 25–47 https://doi.org/10.25256/PAAL.25.1.2.

McGarr, Olliver, and Amanda Maria Clifford. 2013. 'Just enough to make you take it seriously': Exploring students' attitudes towards peer assessment. *Higher Education* 65 (6): 677–693. http://www.jstor.org/stable/23481591.

6.9 Students Teach Students

Goodlad, Sinclair. 1997. Students as tutors and mentors. In *Mentoring and tutoring by students*, ed. Sinclair Goodlad, 1–18. London: Routledge.

Krikorian, Maryann. 2023. Carl Rogers: A person-centered approach. In *The Palgrave handbook of educational thinkers*, ed. Brett A. Geier. Cham: Palgrave Macmillan. https://doi.org/10.1007/978-3-030-81037-5_106-1.

Roscoe, Rod D. 2014. Self-monitoring and knowledge-building in learning by teaching. *Instructional Science* 42: 327–351. https://doi.org/10.1007/s11251-013-9283-4.

Stigmar, Martin. 2016. Peer-to-peer teaching in higher education: A critical literature review. *Mentoring and Tutoring: Partnership in Learning* 24 (2): 124–136. https://doi.org/10.1080/13611267.2016.1178963.

Torshizi, Mehdi Davari, and Mostafa Bahraman. 2019. I explain, therefore I learn: Improving students' assessment literacy and deep learning by teaching. *Studies in Educational Evaluation* 61: 66–73, https://doi.org/10.1016/j.stueduc.2019.03.002.

7

Critiquing Humanism and PPCP, Using PPCP Beyond EAP, Concluding Thoughts

7.1 Overview of the Chapter

Following outlines of humanism in education, EAP contexts and potential profiles of EAP students, this publication then presented its objective—PPCP. This final chapter concludes the publication by looking at the potential limitations arising from this content and is split into four sections. Section 7.2 provides a critique of humanism and this links with Sect. 7.3 which is a critique of PPCP itself. Section 7.4 then considers PPCP's potential application beyond EAP with reference to the activities presented in Chapter 6. The final part of this chapter provides concluding thoughts.

7.2 Critiquing Humanism in Education

It could be said that this publication has taken a one-sided perspective of humanism. That is to say that humanism is a positive approach to education and that its application could prove beneficial to learners. However, there are indeed many arguments that could counter humanistic approaches to education. On reading this publication you may have

L. Dyer, *A Humanistic Approach to English for Academic Purposes Pedagogy*,
https://doi.org/10.1007/978-3-032-00186-3_7

identified multiple issues with the suggestion that EAP needs a humanistic approach to its pedagogy. From this it can be said that there is no doubt that humanism is not the answer to solve all problems faced by EAP learners, nor is it suitable for all EAP contexts. This section briefly discusses a range of points around the use of humanism in educational practices.

1. **Humanism Is a Psychology, Not an Educational Approach**

As highlighted in Chapter 2, the philosophical approach to humanism was largely developed by psychologists. Indeed, two of the key protagonists in Chapter 2—Maslow and Rogers—were both psychologists. Coming from psychology rather than education, humanistic education could be viewed as a psychological experiment to observe human behavioural responses to situations (Willers 1975) rather than focusing on the key aspects of education—the accumulation of knowledge and skills. A humanistic approach to education focuses on achieving the goal of self-actualisation and positivity in feelings (Willers 1975) yet this may be in detriment to academic achievements which continue to be the objective in education as a whole.

However, despite the issues raised above humanistic approaches have been shown to be generally accepted by learners. Student-centred learning in particular has been applied in many contexts globally and has been viewed positively by both teachers and students alike (Benlahcene et al. 2020; Matsuyama et al. 2019; Frambach et al. 2014).

2. **Does Humanism Truly Respect the Individual Learner?**

Humanism is about respecting the individual, yet if a humanistic approach to pedagogy is taken it might not respect all. For example, humanism encourages collaboration but this might go against student inclusivity learning plans which may call for individuals to work independently. Additionally, in Sect. 1.5 it was stated that EAP learners are often moulded into what is the expected academic norm. Humanism itself has the potential to mould learners into its own norms as learners are encouraged to undertake learning in ways that they may not be acquainted with. In this way, students who do not fit the mould may feel in deficit if they are unable to achieve this ideal (Heng 2016). Humanism can also be considered as invasive, coercive and exploitative in its functionality (Stevick 1990). Its invasiveness stems from the fact that it asks students to consider their personal selves in the learning process. The coerciveness comes from being asked to share that personal information with others, be it peers and/or educators. As a result some learners may feel compelled to share this information when they might not want to. Although students may be instructed that they may decline to be involved in activities, social pressures may lead to undesired participation (Brumfit 1982 cited by Stevick 1990). As such students may be 'tamed' into becoming something that they are not (Sloterdijk 1999 cited in Woo 2024). Finally, the exploitativeness comes from the role that the learners take in the learning process, being at the forefront and creating content rather than the teacher taking control and doing a 'teacher's job' in the classroom (see student expectations of the teacher).

But despite the potential issues with humanism, it does still offer the learner an approach that places them at the centre of the learning process. As one of the facets of humanism is to respect one another, teachers may instruct students to participate, collaborate and share as they wish. Pedagogical tasks could be designed so that they can also be completed through non-humanistic approaches to suit the learner.

3. **Humanism Is a Western Philosophy**

As shown in Chapter 2, humanism emerged from Western societies, with particular development coming from mid-twentieth-century white middle-class USA (Pearson and Podeschi 1999). Thus the use of humanistic approaches to education may not be suitable for all contexts, especially those who do not fall into that category. The use of humanistic education may direct learners away from local contextual expectations and may prove to be worthless outside the classroom. For humanism, individualisation is considered a key focus (Pearson and Podeschi 1999) as this is a preferential characteristic in Western cultures. Yet individualisation may not suit the needs of and wants of learners outside a

Western context. Therefore, the use of humanism in education needs to be considered in relation to the learner and their context.

However, what humanism does do is respect. If aspects of it do not fit the learner or the situation, they should not be used. Careful consideration should instead be given to what works for both. This may mean making small appropriate changes to existing practices based on humanism. Or indeed it may raise awareness of the possibility of other approaches to pedagogy that are more suitable for the context and the student.

4. **Academic Disciplines May Continue to Use 'Traditional' Teaching Methods**

Questions may be asked over whether EAP should be taking a humanistic approach if academic disciplines maintain 'traditional' teaching methods. If EAP adopts a humanistic approach to pedagogy, this might be in contrast to pedagogy in academic studies. For example, some academic disciplines may require specific approaches to pedagogy such as disciplinary conventions of teacher-centred approaches in mathematics (Voskoglou 2019) through to the independent self-directives of postgraduate research. If EAP's aim is to prepare the learner for or support the learner in their academic studies, using a humanistic approach might not be reflective of academic studies.

However, as has already been stated in this publication, a PSP EAP is designed to prepare students for academic studies. This does not necessarily require a replication of what takes place in academic studies. In fact, there are many aspects of EAP that do not replicate the characteristics of disciplinary study such as short intensive courses and the amount of teacher support. It can be said that academic disciplines themselves have varying approaches to pedagogy such as aforementioned mathematics, the extensive use of discussion in philosophy (Cahn 2018) and subjects involving practical work such as chemistry and music. Based on this, would EAP need to take an approach that replicates the disciplines? Would it be possible or practical to imitate teaching and learning in each students' future academic studies? As EAP has become a discipline in its own right (see Sect. 1.2) it has the opportunity to develop its own pedagogical approaches.

5. **The Teacher's Expectation of Teaching**

As this book is about pedagogy, the focus has been on the learner. However, for a humanistic approach to education to be successful, it needs to be accepted by the teacher as a means to educate. Yet for many teachers, the humanistic approach may be difficult to accept (Nguyen 2008). A humanistic education calls for the teacher to be the facilitator as opposed to the authority, but this may be challenging for teachers who have existing strategies in place from teaching experience or have received training that does not include humanistic elements. For a teacher to apply humanistic traits to their teaching, they need to be confident in their ability to adapt to this approach (Willers 1975).

However, a humanistic approach may offer the teacher themselves the possibility of their own self-actualisation. Intrigue, enjoyment and belonging all have the potential to influence a teacher's levels of self-actualisation (Arslan 2017) and with these being components of several of the activities in the compendium (see Chapter 6), humanistic education may not only benefit the learner but the educator too as they witness success in their practice.

6. **Humanism and the Notion of Positivity**

As demonstrated through multiple PTAs in Chapter 2, humanism puts positivity at the forefront. PTAs such as Csikszentmihalyi's theory of flow, positive education, affective learning and achievement emotions all promote positive feelings as necessary for success in learning. But what is it that determines positive feelings? Who is it that determines what should be considered a positive and what should be considered a negative? How much positivity is needed for learning to be positive? The general rule for positive psychology is for a person to experience flourishing (Held 2018). Questions can be raised over how this is demonstrated in educational contexts. For instance, for one learner flourishing could be achieving high grades whereas for another it could be having the courage to volunteer an answer in class.

A change of approach is one option that could aid the learning process. This change in approach could lead to a flourishing and allow for the learner to have a more positive experience. A positive learning experience does not always mean a Maslow peak experience, but it is one in which the learner can feel satisfied with the situation they are in. Although there are many ways through which this can be achieved, compassionate actions from educators have been shown to play a role in determining learning positivity (Khanna et al. 2024). Humanism calls for compassionate actions through respect, empathy and enjoyment, thus supporting its use in educational practice.

7. **Humanism Is Outdated**

Chapter 2 demonstrated that those who could be considered significant protagonists in humanistic education (Montessori, Maslow and Rogers) produced their work in the late nineteenth through to the mid twentieth centuries. Whilst the other PTAs presented in the chapter are also significant, it is the work of these three authors that perhaps could be considered the most meaningful. Yet, the dating of their work calls into question the relevance of its application to contemporary educational practices. With increasing digitality in educational practices, more suitable approaches to pedagogy emerge that complement how teaching and learning is evolving. For instance, Sect. 5.5.1 mentioned the non-human as an appearing 'person' in teaching and learning. Through the non-human there is the potential for the role of the teacher to change from humanism's facilitator to a perhaps a supporter of the non-human and director to students on how to use digitality.

Nevertheless, despite being potentially outdated, humanism can still be applied to contemporary education processes. Section 5.2 presented a successful contemporary application of humanism to a pedagogical activity, thus demonstrating it can still be used in the modern classroom.

8. **Humanism Does Not Work for Everyone**

It is important to repeat here that even Rogers states that humanistic approaches to learning, specifically student-centred learning, are not suitable for all (Rogers 2001). A belief that all students are capable of learning through a student-centred approach is inherently wrong (Tangney 2013). Some learners may take a deliberate stance against humanistic approaches whilst others may face challenges in adapting to them. If students have had particular success a specific way of learning and teaching, it should be respected if they wish to continue with that approach (Xu 2022) and not inflict wholescale humanistic pedagogies on them. As humanism is about respecting the human self, it is important that these students' opinions and experiences are respected.

7.3 Critiquing PPCP

This section considers PPCP. As a humanistic theory, immediately questions can be raised as to how humanism, which values and respects the individual, could have a theory. Each of the four components of PPCP are briefly discussed to show that the broadness and interpretation of these components leave space for the educator to tailor them to the individual.

7.3.1 People

As a humanistic theory, people is the first component of PPCP and it is also probably the most coherent. The role of the person is essential to consider in both humanism and PPCP, thus it is essential to consider what role each individual has in an activity. However, as shown, humanism has collaboration conventions and this is demonstrated by the set-up of activities in Chapter 6. Some of these activities function through student collaboration (e.g. listening tag team, paired peer feedback). This calls into question PPCP's potential to truly respect individual learners (see 2. Does humanism truly respect the individual?) as the activities may not be suitable for all learners. To deal with the collaborative aspect of PPCP, rather than it being between students it could be between teacher and student. For example, for both the listening tag team and paired peer feedback the teacher could take on the role of a student by carrying out the directed tasks. The student themselves can use this as a chance not only to demonstrate their existing skills but also as an opportunity for noticing.

7.3.2 Place

Place calls for the teacher to provide learners with multiple locations for activities to take place. Yet the reality for many teachers and learners is that, save for homework tasks, teaching and learning takes place entirely in a physical classroom. The use of digitality and hybrid/blending learning may not be an option, thus placing restrictions on specific actions such as maintaining anonymity (see Sect. 7.3.4). Furthermore, care should also be taken over which places are in use. In my own teaching practice, the use of digital platforms without sufficient training led to negative for several students as they attempted to learn their use at the same time as completing the task I had set them. This issue could have been resolved through better training or by asking learners to use a different place that was more familiar to them.

7.3.3 Compassion

This component could be considered as being perhaps the broadest in the theory. As shown in Sect. 5.5.3, multiple factors could constitute compassion, with suggestions being time, adjusting the learning environment and anonymisation. In Sect. 5.5.3.3 it was suggested that time might not need to be applied to learning activities. However, this may be considered unrealistic due to the intensive nature of education. For the EAP student in receipt of a visa or scholarship it is likely that there are externally designated requirements to achieve in a specific timeframe. Therefore, it is necessary that the student undergoes training to acquire the necessary requisites during that time spell. As such, the removal of time or timings for pedagogical activities may not be practical in order to complete all training that is deemed necessary.

Moving on adjustments to the learning environment, in several instances in the compendium of activities (Chapter 6) it is stated that the place aspect of the activity should be one that is 'conducive to learning' or likewise. Questions can be asked over what is deemed to be a conducive learning environment. Whilst a move towards student-centred learning environments is generally seen as a positive (Lundberg and Stigmar 2023), it may not be possible to have this type of set up. However, as shown in Sect. 5.5.3.2 there are many ways to make adjustments to the learning environments with infrastructural elements such as ventilation and temperature (Haverinen-Shaughnessy and Shaugnessy 2015) can play a role in improving student comfort and performance.

The final suggestion put forward for compassion is anonymisation. Conditions in the learning environment may not make this possible, such as students being in close proximity when discussing the work of their peers. Students may also be required to identify themselves in all of their work, questioning the possibility of using anonymity. Following the principles of humanism, anonymisation should only be used if it is acceptable in the context.

7.3.4 Power

The final aspect of PPCP proposes that if the previous three come together successfully then the learner will have 'power'. Yet, what is it that determines 'power'? How is 'power' measured? Perhaps the most obvious indicator for power is academic output measured by grades, with higher grades signifying success (Kahu and Nelson 2017). Yet there are other means to measure power. Potential markers for power could be the student demonstrating a higher level of confidence in their speaking, increased willingness to participate in learning activities and deeper levels of criticality in their work. Is it possible that the application of humanistic principles to pedagogy would create such possibilities for learners? Additionally, although this component is called 'power', the fact that a teacher is still required to orchestrate the management of pedagogical activities (Dillenbourg 2013) means that learners do not have full power over their learning.

However, my own experience outlined in Sect. 5.2 showed that the use of humanistic pedagogy can have an empowering effect on learners.

Although this was just one select group of students who had a mass light-bulb experience, subsequent applications of humanistic approaches to my own teaching practices demonstrate that humanism could provide leverage in student empowerment.

7.4 PPCP's Application Beyond EAP

This section reviews PPCP's potential application beyond the field of EAP. It does this by briefly reviewing PPCP's construct before providing an overview of the compendium of activities and their potential transfer beyond EAP. Although PPCP was designed in an EAP context, its generalisability, such as not pinpointing exact features of EAP in its structure, means that there is potential for impact across a range of fields (Evans et al. 2020). This notion of generalisability also draws attention to the ease of adapting PPCP to non-EAP pedagogies.

PPCP was designed for the designing and planning of pedagogical activities for EAP students. It was in response to issues reported by EAP students and through my own observations and experiences of working with these students. It was therefore initially intended as theory solely for EAP practitioners. However, on reflection it is clear that PPCP could also be applied to pedagogical activities in non-EAP contexts. This is because PPCP is a humanistic theory that takes into account how the learner learns but not, save for the academic studies exploration, what they learn. This means that PPCP could be applied by teaching professionals of disciplines other than EAP. PPCP is not a theory just for EAP and this can be supported by reviewing the elements that make up the theory—people, place, compassion and power. None of these elements explicitly refers to language acquisition, purpose A of EAP outlined in Sect. 1.3. When considering purpose B of EAP, that of developing academic skills, it could be said that the 'power' aspect is the enhancement of those skills and therefore PPCP can be linked to this aspect of EAP. It can also be argued that purpose C of EAP—community skills—is also potentially achieved through PPCP. Whilst I have suggested that community skills should be a purpose of EAP, these skills could be considered pertinent to all academic disciplines meaning that PPCP can be applied outside EAP.

7.4.1 Discussion on Compendium Activities

This next section reviews the eight activities presented in the compendium in Chapter 6 and discusses their potential use beyond EAP. The eight activities presented in the compendium were:

- Academic studies exploration
- Conversation sessions
- Dialogic presentation
- Intercultural rhetoric as a foundation
- Learner vs. AI
- Listening tag team
- Paired peer feedback
- Students teach students

Academic Studies Exploration

EAP is for the most part taken in preparation for academic studies. For many undertaking EAP courses, their future academic studies serve as a target for their ideal self, one in which can carry out disciplinary studies through the English language. Through the academic studies exploration learners can gain an understanding of their future programmes of study. However, non-EAP students may also benefit from this activity, especially for those courses in which students may have limited or no prior knowledge and time should be spent fostering disciplinary understandings (Quality Assurance Agency for Higher Education 2019).

Conversation Sessions

Although a key mode of assessment and teaching and learning in education, oral skills have been sidelined in favour of other skills such as writing (Heron et al. 2022). However, there is no doubt that oracy can play a key role in learning successes. Students should be supported in developing their verbal communication skills and this support should not just be restricted to those acquiring language (Heron et al. 2022). HE in general separates the L1 and non-L1 speakers to provide support that can be considered bespoke to their needs. Yet it has been shown that these two groups actually have similar needs and meaning that this separation should not take place as both groups require training in 'speaking skills' (Dippold et al. 2019). Oral communication is highly valued in employability terms (Heron 2019) so providing opportunities for all students to practice and develop spoken skills can enhance skillsets for the navigating of different contexts (Heron et al. 2022). Providing opportunities to converse on topics relevant disciplines could support the development of oracy skills for all students.

Dialogic Presentation

The dialogic presentation was created for EAP students who had the task of presenting in their L2 on top of negotiating the other barriers they may perceive to be present. However, as presentations are a common feature of many university curricula (Simpson et al. 2019), there is need to consider how this task may affect even L1 speakers of English as it is not just language which can impact on performance (Bhati 2012). Therefore, the dialogic presentation has potential transferability and can reach a wider market than just EAP. As it consists of only three changes to the traditional presentation—presenters and audience sitting down together, a small audience and the audience asking questions throughout the presentation—it could be seen as being relatively adaptable across a range of teaching and learning contexts.

Intercultural Rhetoric *as a Foundation*

Of all of the compendium activities, it is this one that has the strongest connection to EAP. This is because it asks learners to review and compare similarities and differences between rhetorics their language and English, thus directly addressing purpose A of EAP. In this activity learners can make use of translanguaging and existing knowledge and skills to aid their EAP acquisition. However intercultural rhetoric can be used outside EAP, one such example being with language learning in general (Liu and Du 2018). It can also be argued that this activity can go beyond even language learning disciplines. Even a group of L1 speakers of English could be tasked with reflecting on their knowledge and skills of how language is used in different written contexts. Thus this activity could be transferred to non-EAP contexts.

Learner vs. AI

At the time of writing this publication, AI is an emerging technology which has begun to be integrated into teaching and learning. However, it is recognised that AI does have its limitations and may not be able to produce effective outputs, not simply in terms of language but also content (Borger et al. 2023). For these reasons, it can be beneficial for students to identify the gaps that AI may have and 'take on' the computer to highlight both its strengths and weaknesses (Fong et al. 2022). Providing students with a learner vs. AI task can be applied to many disciplines. Training in AI can also enhance employability potential as it demonstrates a learner's capability to adapt to evolving digitality (Nartey 2024). Therefore, the learner vs. AI activity could be applied to non-EAP contexts.

Listening Tag Team

Multiple factors could come into play in determining success in listening to lectures, not only the language that they are delivered in, such as digital distractions and losing concentration (Zureick et al. 2018). Therefore, it can be said that finding potential alternatives to mitigating this issue is potent to a range of disciplines. The listening tag team is a possible activity that students in any discipline may use when listening to lectures.

Paired Peer Feedback

As stated in the compendium, peer feedback is a highly valuable tool that has the potential for many learners, including non-EAP students, to gain a deeper understanding of the assessment and feedback process. Peer feedback is used as a method of feedback for many pedagogical activities for students to acknowledge what has been achieved and what could be improved (Sackstein 2017). Paired peer feedback could be used to mitigate the possibility of producing or receiving negative or uncomfortable feedback. Paired peer feedback could be applied to any pedagogical activity in which peer feedback is required.

Students Teach Students

This activity, which may also be referred to as peer teaching, requires a student who is not a professional teacher to teach fellow students. This activity can aid the learning of both the 'teacher' and the recipients, not only through the delivery of content but also through the process of preparing and delivering the teaching material. This activity allows for 'teacher' personalisation and autonomy in their creation of teaching material which in turn can enhance intrinsic motivation (Nshimiyimana and Cartledge 2020). It can therefore increase the possibility of a positive learning outcome through a positive psychology. For the recipients, this approach may also prove beneficial as strategies may differ from regular teachers which may lead to more engagement from the recipients (Tanga and Luggya 2020). Students teach students could be used across a wide range of non-EAP disciplines.

7.5 Summary of Key Points Raised in This Publication

Chapter 1 of this publication introduced the topic humanistic education and its potential use in EAP. It began with an example pedagogical activity and discussed how this activity might not enable the student to demonstrate their true academic potential. It then provided a brief outline of the evolution of EAP. It outlined the three purposes of EAP which are to develop language skills, academic skills and community skills for academic studies.

Chapter 2 provided an outline of humanism, its definitions and its application to education. It highlighted the range of PTAs and their importance to the field. It demonstrated that although each of the PTAs could be considered humanistic, they focused on a variety of different aspects. This chapter considered the ideas from these PTAs could be applied to EAP.

Chapter 3 presented a range of contexts in which EAP takes place. These contexts were divided into four main groups—physical, content, construct and demographic. These contexts were divided further into eleven subgroups. With each subgroup was a deliberation as to how these might impact on EAP and its pedagogy. The chapter considered how each of these contexts may influence the approach to EAP pedagogy employed.

Chapter 4 outlined a range of EAP student profiles. It did this by considering emotions in EAP, why the student has chosen to undertake EAP, their chosen place of study, the students who might study in the contexts presented in Chapter 3 and finally barriers to EAP study. The purpose of this chapter was to highlight the EAP student's journey and that a range of external factors could influence their learning experience and potential outcomes. Due to these factors, an alternative approach to pedagogy should be taken to teaching EAP students to provide a more compassion learning experience.

Chapter 5 presented PPCP theory. This was done in both visual and written form. The visual showed how the three teacher driven components—people, place and compassion—were linked to the student driven component—power. The written form presented features of each of the components of PPCP and how these could be viewed in relation to pedagogy. This chapter provided examples of elements from each of the components that the teacher could consider in pedagogy.

Chapter 6 was the compendium of activities. The activities demonstrated how PPCP can be applied to existing pedagogical activities and that even through minor amendments these activities can be approached in a more compassionate way. It also presented activities that were made from scratch using PPCP. This variety of activities shows PPCP's versatility and flexibility in its application to pedagogical activities. Each of the activities was linked to at least one of the PTAs presented in Chapter 2.

7.6 Concluding Thoughts

PPCP should be considered as a paradigm. It is not a perfect framework for the creation of EAP pedagogy. Instead it should be seen as a loose structure to raise awareness of factors which may affect student emotions and consequently may impact on their performance. The components are broad and should, where possible, be interpreted and applied to suit the needs of learners. PPCP does not seek to replace any existing pedagogical approaches to EAP, rather it aims to support them. Moreover, a full-scale implementation of PPCP will not be applicable to every EAP context and consideration for even one component might not be feasible. You may find that PPCP does not work for your students. They may be used to prefer or perform better under other approaches. You may also find PPCP does not suit your own teaching practice or meet the requirements set by course governance. Nevertheless, PPCP can give students a chance to achieve their potential at a micro and macro level and as practitioners it is our duty to give them that chance if possible. Making even the smallest adjustment to the learning experience through the application of PPCP could prove beneficial for learners. For those practitioners who have some level of control over their practices, recognition of students as individuals navigating their own EAP journeys should be taken into account during the EAP learning process.

Finally, at the beginning of this publication I asked you to consider the situation of Lee and Jo in the presentation and feedback activity. After reading this publication, you may choose to offer Lee a dialogic presentation and Jo to provide feedback through paired peer feedback. However, this decision would need to be based on the individual students in question, the learning context and the amount of flexibility you may have as a practitioner in determining learning activities.

In the spirit of humanism, opinions of PPCP are respected as PPCP is a suggestion you may wish to use. However, I hope that by reading this publication there is an increased awareness of how making changes to existing pedagogical activities or creating new ones can have a positive impact on the student learning experience.

References

Arslan, Ali. 2017. Basic needs as a predictors of prospective teachers' self-actualization. *Universal Journal of Educational Research* 5 (6): 1045–1050. https://eric.ed.gov/?id=EJ1143893.

Benlahcene, Abderrahim, Sana Anwar Lashari, Tahira Anwar Lashari, Muhammad Waleed Shehzad, and Wu Deli. 2020. Exploring the perception of students using student-centered learning approach in a Malaysian public university. *International Journal of Higher Education* 9 (1): 204–217. https://eric.ed.gov/?id=EJ1240462.

Bhati, Shyam S. 2012. The effectiveness of oral presentation assessment in a finance subject: an empirical examination. *Journal of University Teaching & Learning Practice* 9 (2): 6 https://files.eric.ed.gov/fulltext/EJ984907.pdf.

Borger, Jessica G., Ashley P. Ng, Holly Anderton, George W. Ashdown, Megan Auld, Marnie E. Blewitt, Daniel V. Brown, Melissa J. Call, Peter Collins, Saskia Freytag, Leonard C. Harrison, Eva Hesping, Jaci Hoysted, Anna Johnston, Andrew McInneny, Phil Tang, Lachlan Whitehead, Aaron Jex, and Shalin H. Naik. 2023. Artificial intelligence takes center stage: Exploring the capabilities and implications of ChatGPT and other AI-assisted technologies in scientific research and education. *Immunology and Cell Biology* 101 (10): 923–935. https://doi.org/10.1111/imcb.12689.

Cahn, Steven M. 2018. *Teaching philosophy: A guide*. New York: Routledge.

Dillenbourg, Pierre. 2013. Design for classroom orchestration. *Computers and Education* 69: 485–492. https://doi.org/10.1016/j.compedu.2013.04.013.

Dippold, Doris, Stephanie Bridges, Sue Eccles, and Emma Mullen. 2019. Taking ELF off the shelf: Developing HE students' speaking skills through a focus on English as a lingua franca. *Linguistics and Education* 54: 1–10. https://doi.org/10.1016/j.linged.2019.100761.

Evans, Carol, Camille Kandiko Howson, Alex Forsythe, and Corony Edwards. 2020. What constitutes high quality higher education pedagogical research? *Assessment & Evaluation in Higher Education* 46 (4): 525–546. https://doi.org/10.1080/02602938.2020.1790500.

Fong, Alvis C., Ajay K. Gupta, Steve M. Carr, Shameek Bhattacharjee, and Michael Harnar. 2022. A balanced pedagogical approach toward AI readiness education for STEM learners: Instilling a balanced view of AI capabilities through active learning in both traditional classroom and self-directed online environments In *Proceedings of the 2022 6th International Conference on Education and E-Learning*, 260–266. https://doi.org/10.1145/3578837.3578875.

Frambach, Janneke M., Erik W. Driessen, Philip Beh, and Cees P.M. van der Vleuten 2014. Quiet or questioning? Students' discussion behaviors in student-centered education across cultures. *Studies in Higher Education* 39 (6): 1001–1021. https://doi.org/10.1080/03075079.2012.754865.

Haverinen-Shaughnessy, Ulla, and Richard J. Shaughnessy. 2015. Effects of classroom ventilation rate and temperature on students' test scores. *PLoS ONE* 10 (8): e0136165–e0136165. https://doi.org/10.1371/journal.pone.0136165.

Held, Barbara S. 2018. Positive psychology's a priori problem. *The Journal of Humanistic Psychology* 58 (3): 313–342. https://doi.org/10.1177/0022167817739409.

Heng, Tang T. 2016. Different is not deficient: Contradicting stereotypes of Chinese international students in US higher education. *Studies in Higher Education* 43 (1): 22–36. https://doi.org/10.1080/03075079.2016.1152466.

Heron, Marion. 2019. Making the case for oracy skills in higher education: practices and opportunities. *Journal of University Teaching and Learning Practice* 16 (2): 9. https://doi.org/10.53761/1.16.2.2.

Heron, Marion, Sally Baker, Karen Gravett, and Evonne Irwin. 2022. Scoping academic oracy in higher education: Knotting together forgotten connections to equity and academic literacies. *Higher Education Research & Development* 42 (1): 62–77. https://doi.org/10.1080/07294360.2022.2048635.

Kahu, Ella R., and Karen Nelson. 2017. Student engagement in the educational interface: Understanding the mechanisms of student success. *Higher Education Research & Development* 37 (1): 58–71. https://doi.org/10.1080/07294360.2017.1344197.

Khanna, Monica, Isaac Jacob, and Anjali Chopra. 2024. Marketing of higher education institutes through the creation of positive learning experiences—Analyzing the role of teachers' caring behaviors. *Journal of Marketing for Higher Education* 34 (1): 116–135. https://doi.org/10.1080/08841241.2021.1966158.

Liu, Ying, and Qian Du. 2018. Intercultural rhetoric through a learner lens: American students' perceptions of evidence use in Chinese yìlùnwén writing. *Journal of Second Language Writing* 40: 1–11. https://doi.org/10.1016/j.jslw.2018.01.001.

Lundberg, Adrian, and Martin Stigmar. 2023. University teachers' shifting views of successful learning environments in the future. *Scandinavian Journal of Educational Research* 67 (6): 964–979. https://doi.org/10.1080/00313831.2022.2115127.

Matsuyama, Yasushi, Motoyuki Nakaya, Hitoaki Okazaki, Adam Jon Lebowitz, J. Jimmie Leppink, and Cees van der Vleuten. 2019. Does changing from a teacher-centered to a learner-centered context promote self-regulated learning: A qualitative study in a Japanese undergraduate setting. *BMC Medical Education* 19 (1): 152–152. https://doi.org/10.1186/s12909-019-1550-x.

Nartey, Emmanuel K. 2024. Guiding principles of generative AI for employability and learning in UK universities. *Cogent Education* 11 (1): 2357898. https://doi.org/10.1080/2331186X.2024.2357898.

Nguyen, Phương-Mai. 2008. *Culture and cooperation: Cooperative learning in Asian Confucian heritage cultures. The case of Viet Nam.* Phd thesis, Utrecht University. https://dspace.library.uu.nl/handle/1874/27818.

Nshimiyimana, Alexis, and Peter Thomas Cartledge. 2020. Peer-teaching at the University of Rwanda—A qualitative study based on self-determination theory. *BMC Medical Education* 20 (1): 230–230. https://doi.org/10.1186/s12909-020-02142-0.

Pearson, Elaine M., and Ronald L. Podeschi. 1999. Humanism and individualism: Maslow and his critics. *Adult Education Quarterly* 50 (1): 41–55. https://doi.org/10.1177/07417139922086902.

Quality Assurance Agency for Higher Education. 2019. *Subject benchmark: History of art, architecture and design,* Gloucester, Quality Assurance Agency for Higher Education. https://www.qaa.ac.uk/docs/qaa/subject-benchmark-statements/subject-benchmark-statement-history-of-art-architecture-and-design.pdf?sfvrsn=2ff0a181_6.

Rogers, Carl R. 2001. The interpersonal relationship in the facilitation of learning. In *Supporting lifelong learning,* eds. Julia Clarke, Ann Hanson, Roger Harrison, and Fiona Reeve, 36–50. London: Routledge. https://www.perlego.com/book/1602283.

Sackstein, Starr 2017. *Peer feedback in the classroom: Empowering students to be the experts.* Alexandra, Virginia: ASCD.

Simpson, Tmothy, Kathryn Holden, Deborah Merrick, Simon Dawson, and Lynn Bedford. 2019. Does video feedback and peer observation offer a valid method of reinforcing oral presentation training for undergraduate biochemists? *Higher Education Pedagogies* 4 (1): 262–283. https://doi.org/10.1080/23752696.2019.1587717.

Stevick, Earl W. 1990. *Humanism in language teaching*. Oxford: Oxford University Press.

Tanga, Magdaline, and Simon Luggya. 2020. Teaching and learning in a South African University: Are peer facilitators' strategies Succeeding? *Journal of Academic Ethics* 20: 3–22. https://doi.org/10.1007/s10805-020-09361-6.

Tangney, Sue. 2013. Student-centred learning: A humanist perspective. *Teaching in Higher Education* 19 (3): 266–275. https://doi.org/10.1080/13562517.2013.860099.

Voskoglou, Michael. 2019. Comparing teaching methods of mathematics at university level. *Education Sciences* 9 (3): 204. https://doi.org/10.3390/educsci9030204.

Willers, Jack Conrad. 1975. Humanistic education: Concepts, criteria and criticism. *Peabody Journal of Education* 53 (1): 39–44. http://www.jstor.org/stable/1491821.

Woo, Jeong-Gil. 2024. Rethinking humanism and education through Sloterdijk's rules for the human Zoo. *Studies in Philosophy and Education* 43: 223–241. https://doi.org/10.1007/s11217-024-09932-9.

Xu, Jinqi. 2022. Memorisation is not rote learning: Rethinking memorisation as an embodied practice for Chinese students. *Journal of Multilingual and Multicultural Development* 45 (9): 3963–3979. https://doi.org/10.1080/01434632.2022.2134878.

Zureick, Andrew H., Jesse Burk-Rafel, Joel A. Purkiss, and Michael Hortsch. 2018. The interrupted learner: How distractions during live and video lectures influence learning outcomes. *Anatomical Sciences Education* 11 (4): 366–376. https://doi.org/10.1002/ase.1754.

Index

L. Dyer, *A Humanistic Approach to English for Academic Purposes Pedagogy*, https://doi.org/10.1007/978-3-032-00186-3

FSC
www.fsc.org
MIX
Papier | Fördert gute Waldnutzung
FSC® C083411

Kolibri 360 GmbH
Ferdinand-Jühlke-Straße 7
99095 Erfurt, Deutschland
produktsicherheit@kolibri360.de